Racial Conflict in Contemporary Society

John Stone

Fontana Press/Collins

First published in 1985 by Fontana Paperbacks and William Collins,
8 Grafton Street, London W1X 3LA

Hardback ISBN 0 00 197173–5
Paperback ISBN 0 00 686016–8

Copyright © John Stone 1985

Printed and bound in Great Britain by
Billing & Sons Ltd, Worcester

Fontana Press is an imprint of
Fontana Paperbacks, a division of
the Collins Publishing Group

for Alana

Contents

Acknowledgements   8

1 Race relations without races?   9

2 Minority groups and power   34

3 Race relations and class   62

4 Race relations and social change   83

5 Race relations and social institutions   110

6 The quest for racial justice   136

Notes   159

Bibliography   167

Index   187

Acknowledgements

The extent to which I have made use of the theories and research of others in formulating the ideas expressed in this book will be apparent to any reader. The degree to which I differ from many of these writers exonerates them all from any responsibility for the views put forward here. I would particularly like to thank colleagues at Columbia, Oxford and London for innumerable provocative discussions over the years. My debt to the following scholars and friends can be judged by the frequent references to their ideas (that I hope are not too grossly misrepresented!) appearing throughout the book. These include Hans van Amersfoort, Don Baker, Michael Banton, Pierre van den Berghe, Walker Connor, Leo Kuper, Barbara Lal, Alan Little, Bob Miles, Vernon Reynolds, John Rex, Tony Richmond, Judith Shapiro and Anthony Smith. I would like to add a special word of appreciation to Kenneth Kirkwood, whose Thursday morning seminars have been a constant source of stimulation, and to the Warden and fellows of St Antony's for electing me to an associate fellowship thereby enabling me to continue my long and happy connection with the college. This book was originally commissioned for the Fontana New Sociology series, edited by Gavin Mackenzie. Without his enthusiastic and patient encouragement the book would never have been completed. My greatest debt remains, as always, to Roleen who has had to suffer the consequences of yet another project.

1 Race relations without races?

It was only after the end of the Second World War, and particularly during the 1960s, that social scientists began to recognize the central place of race relations in the study of society. Why was this crucial area of human relationships regarded for so long as marginal to the mainstream of sociological analysis? The most convincing answer to this question is that which emphasizes the change in the balance of world power which took place during the second half of the twentieth century (Tinker, 1977). Since the era of colonial expansion, European states had dominated the rest of the world, while within the metropolitan societies racial conflicts appeared to be largely insignificant. All this changed during the course of the present century, but by then the foundations of modern social theory had already been firmly established on the basis of class conflicts engendered by nascent capitalist industry and political conflicts emanating from the upheavals following the French Revolution. Race and ethnic issues were left out of the agenda as a result of the immediate, ethnocentric preoccupations of the founding fathers of modern sociology.

By the middle of the twentieth century, this position was becoming increasingly untenable. The independence of India in 1948 and the establishment of the United Nations, with its growing multiracial membership, marked the end of a period in which differences in colour or 'race' roughly corresponded to the division between the powerful and powerless nations and states.[1] Following the lead set by Nkrumah's Ghana in 1957, decolonization in Africa, and the intensifying conflict over apartheid in Southern Africa, reinforced this trend, combining to increase awareness of and sensitivity to the importance of racial and ethnic divisions in the modern world.[2]

At the same time as this fundamental reorganization of the international political scene, major social developments within the most powerful states were working in a similar direction. In the United States, the Civil Rights movement was gathering momentum, challenging the legal basis of racial discrimination and achieving a certain measure of success with the crucial judgement in *Brown versus the Board of Education* (1954), when the Supreme Court declared that the segregationist doctrine of 'separate but equal' was inherently unequal. By the late 1960s, the legal framework for the assault on racialism in American society had been established and the pressure for change shifted away from the rights of minority groups towards their actual levels of achievement. Minority activists and their allies split into a number of factions advocating different strategies to bridge this gap between theory and reality. Some groups stressed the importance of firm political commitment to secure the enforcement of Federal anti-discrimination measures and to promote greater equality in education and employment by means of affirmative action programmes. Others felt that the fundamental need was to raise the level of group consciousness and self-esteem as a vital ingredient in the development of minority power. Still others advocated a more extreme separation from the wider society, with separatist groups, like the Black Muslims, attracting much attention but little mass support.[3]

The example set by blacks in America was soon followed by other oppressed minorities, such as the Chicanos, Puerto Ricans and American Indians. It was also taken up, significantly from a political point of view, by the 'white ethnics', mainly Americans from Italian, Irish, Polish and Greek backgrounds. These events forced social scientists to recognize that the nature of American society, and its impact on different ethnic and racial groups, was considerably more complicated than many had previously assumed. The theory of the 'melting pot', the idea that a nation of immigrants was being transformed into a single new culture and way of life, was attacked as the naive acceptance of a dominant ideology rather than as a careful description of the ethnic reality of contemporary society. However, what theory to put in its place was a much more controversial question. The apparent resurgence of ethnicity was seen by certain analysts as the arrival of a new social category (Glazer & Moynihan, 1975); heralded by others as the recognition of a continuing social reality (Greeley & Jacobsen, 1978); and dismissed by yet others as a purely symbolic phenomenon, an 'ethnicity of last resort' (Gans, 1979). Sociologists were divided in their interpretation of these trends, but not about the importance of the issues that they raised.

In Europe, the labour demands of the postwar economy attracted increasing flows of migrants. Those countries with strong economic links to their former colonies, such as Britain and France, tended to recruit from these areas: the former from the West Indies and the Indian subcontinent; the latter from West Africa, Algeria, the French Caribbean and Vietnam. For countries with weaker colonial ties or no colonial tradition at all, such as Germany or Switzerland, similar needs were met by the *Gastarbeiter* (guest worker) movements from states or regions on the periphery of the European Economic Community, such as Portugal, southern Italy, Morocco and Turkey (Castles & Kosack, 1973; Rist, 1979). At first these immigrants made few demands, they were usually single male workers who had left their families in their countries of origin. They took over low status jobs during an era of low unemployment, and were confined to the 'twilight zones' of British cities (Rex & Moore, 1967) and the *bidonvilles*, shanty towns outside the main French industrial conurbations (Dignan, 1981). The situation was to change dramatically throughout the 1970s and early 1980s, with the rise of unemployment to levels not experienced since the Great Depression and the emergence of a locally born, second generation of black Europeans who had very different expectations from those of their parents. While these new arrivals challenged the assumption of the homogeneity of European 'nation-states' from the outside, the revival of regional and linguistic minorities – such as the Basques and Catalans in Spain; the Scots, Welsh and Irish in Britain; and the Bretons, Occitans and Corsicans in France – attacked it from within (Esman, 1977; Hall, 1979).

The increased salience of racial and ethnic conflict was not confined to North America and Western Europe. The trend appeared to be universal. Socialist societies suffered from ethnic divisions similar to those of the capitalist West, and Stalin's famous dictum – 'nationalist in form; socialist in content' – seemed, on many occasions, to be an ironic reversal of the truth. There was mounting evidence of resentment towards the dominance of ethnic Russians in the Soviet Union where that group made up a bare fifty per cent of the population in a truly multinational state. A continued exodus of Soviet Jews indicated that traditional anti-Semitism, rather than anti-Zionism, may have been one of the Tsarist legacies that the communists had not totally rejected. China, the other great centre of the communist world, was ethnically more homogeneous than the USSR, but within its vast population were some forty million non-Han minorities, concentrated in sensitive locations on the historically disputed borders of the country (Dreyer, 1976). The massive, officially ordered migrations of Han Chinese into these border regions seemed to be motivated by an ethnic calculation, rather than according to Marxist-Leninist, or even Maoist, principles. In South East Asia, conflicts between Vietnam and Cambodia had less to do with rival versions of communist ideology and rather more with long-standing, national enmities. And in the non-communist countries of the region, such as Malaysia, Indonesia or the Philippines, divisions between the indigenous communities and Chinese and Indian minorities, or between Christians and Muslims, continued to threaten the integrity of the state (Lee, 1983).

The abolition of white, colonial rule in independent Africa did not secure the new states from internal cleavages of a profound and dangerous kind (Wai, 1978). In fact, the removal of the colonial power, which had so often promoted ethnic divisions and rivalries as part of the strategy of divide and rule, left behind a crippling legacy of intergroup tension and communal mistrust (Sithole, 1980). The uneven development of different regions, education policies that had favoured particular ethnic and tribal groups, merchant minorities which had been introduced to fill intermediary commercial and bureaucratic roles in the colonial economy, and the selection of the so-called 'martial races' to monopolize the military and policing functions of the empire, combined to place an ethnic curse on so many post-colonial regimes (Kirk-Greene, 1980). What is more, the almost universal adoption of the colonial boundaries of the continent, under the sacrosanct principle of 'national' sovereignty,[4] produced a remarkably arbitrary ethnic lottery and set in motion a continuing tension between nations and states.

This catalogue of ethnic and racial conflict should also include societies such as Canada and Australia which had traditionally perceived their diversity to be the result of linguistic and cultural difference. In these states an increasingly complicated set of new and revived divisions emerged during the postwar period. Canada not only witnessed the resurgence of Quebec nationalism, *la révolution tranquille* of the 1960s, but also saw the stirring of discontent among Indians and Metis, infusions of southern Europeans into the cities of Ontario and Quebec, and the arrival of immigrants and refugees from Asia and Africa which added a colourful diversity to the 'vertical mosaic' (Richmond, 1984). Similar changes were taking place in Australia, with the dismantling of the 'white Australia' policy, the revival of Aboriginal protest, and the steady growth of multiculturalism in education and the mass media (Tatz, 1980). While in New Zealand long-dormant tensions between Maoris and Pakehas began to reawaken over the crucial issue of land ownership and its use (Kawharu, 1977; Cleave, 1979).

As a result of the sheer range, variety and ubiquity of racial and ethnic conflict, only social scientists with the most insensitive sociological imaginations, or those blinkered by a model of society that, by definition, precluded the categories of racial and ethnic group as significant factors in social change, could deny the importance of these developments. It is true that in many of the countries of Latin America, or in the predominantly homogeneous society of Japan, it could be reasonably argued that race and ethnicity were not the most salient sources of social and political conflict. In the former, a highly complex kaleidoscope of race, ethnicity, class and status relationships produced patterns that were rather different from the rest of the world, although the plight of the Indians of the Amazon basin (Morin, 1982), or the communal tensions in Guyana between citizens of African and East Indian descent (Hope & St Pierre, 1983), were by no means unique to the continent. Japan's 'invisible race', the Burakumin (de Vos & Wagatsuma, 1966), raised all manner of fascinating sociological questions concerning the identification of despised minority groups, while the prejudice and discrimination against the Koreans fell into an entirely conventional framework of immigrant deprivation (Lee & de Vos, 1982).

Despite these interesting variations, postwar societies, and hence sociologists trying to understand and write about them, have had to come to terms with a high level of racial and ethnic strife. It has become increasingly clear that modern warfare and other forms of communal violence are partly caused by, and, in turn, have a profound effect upon divisions of race and ethnicity (Smith, 1981a). The terrible history of genocide in the twentieth century provides gruesome support for the belief that such destructive tendencies may owe something to deep-seated, 'primordial' attachments, rather than to entirely rational calculations of material advantage (Kuper, 1981). For it is one thing to propose an economic theory of anti-Semitism, quite another to demonstrate a purely economic logic behind the policy that resulted in millions of Jews being condemned to death in the concentration camps of Auschwitz and Belsen.[5] This is not to claim that economic factors can be discounted altogether; often they are the most important influences shaping race and ethnic relations, and they are rarely insignificant. As I argue in a later chapter, economics and race relations are intimately linked together, but the attempt to apportion relative weights to particular causal variables is an empirical matter, not a theoretical issue, and has to be decided by considering the evidence in each particular case. The balance is a question of measurement rather than metaphysics.

Some social scientists began to move to the other extreme and argued that racial and ethnic divisions were becoming the most important source of social conflict, eclipsing in their magnitude and severity the traditional cleavages of class, status and political power. Andrew Greeley, one of the leading celebrants of the 'new ethnicity' in America during the 1970s, summed up this approach in the following, somewhat polemical, statement:

In a world of nuclear energy, the jet engine, the computer, and the rationalized organization, the principal conflicts are not ideological but tribal . . . the failure of both capitalism and socialism to deliver on their promises of economic prosperity for all are responsible for the tensions both in Eastern Europe and between black and white in the United States. Men were promised affluence and dignity if they yielded their primordial ties. They now suspect that the promise was an empty one and are returning to those primordial ties with a vengeance. (1974:14)

Not all sociologists viewed these developments with the same enthusiasm, and some, like Orlando Patterson, deplored what they saw as the revival of 'ethnic chauvinism', a narrow and dangerous trend that threatened the universal and tolerant values of a liberal society (Patterson, 1977). Of course, it is difficult to make dogmatic generalizations about the social consequences of heightened racial and ethnic consciousness, or about the political implications of ethnic mobilization, for so much depends on the context within which particular policies are pursued. Racial separation in South Africa might have been justified during certain periods in the nineteenth century as an attempt to stop white encroachment on African lands, but the policy of apartheid in the second half of the twentieth century has no such benign motivation. It is simply a rationalization for racial oppression dressed up in the language of group rights (Stone, 1973). Similarly, 'universalistic' criteria have been employed to justify policies designed to undermine the fragile, communal societies of the American Indians or the Australian Aborigines, a thinly disguised ploy to gain access to protected land and mineral rights (Tatz, 1983). Thus apartheid and 'policy space', the term used by Frances Svensson to describe the degree of defensive separation necessary to preserve communal societies from total destruction, might appear, at a superficial level, to be similar strategies. In reality, the motivation behind them and their consequences for the less powerful groups concerned are diametrically opposed (Svensson, 1978). In a slightly different context, a narrow and a historical version of 'universalism' has also been used to attack affirmative action programmes, designed to compensate for a legacy of racial exclusion, and to label them as simply 'reversed racism', or, more politely, affirmative discrimination (Glazer, 1975).

So while the interpretation of the 'ethnic revival' and the heightened state of racial consciousness is a subject of bitter controversy, few of the participants in the debate disagree about its basic relevance. Only, perhaps, William J. Wilson in his ambiguously titled book *The Declining Significance of Race* argues that class, rather than racial factors, is becoming the dominant source of division *within* the American black community. But this interesting thesis does not deny the continuing importance of racialism and ethnic discrimination in American society as a whole (Wilson, 1978). Wilson is merely exposing the complex interaction of race and class in the United States. Above all, he emphasizes the crucial divisions within the black population between a significant middle-class sector and an 'underclass' trapped in the ghetto, suffering from an increasingly intractable tangle of deprivation, and being successively isolated not only from the dominant white society but also from upwardly mobile blacks.

However, sociologists confronted by the pressing reality of

racial and ethnic conflict were faced by an immediate dilemma. The sociological tradition stands opposed to an analysis of social relations in terms of biological factors. Yet the central feature of race relations appears, to the man in the street, to be based on a biological assumption: that mankind can be divided into a number of genetically distinct categories that can be called 'races'. Most biologists and physical anthropologists have had profound doubts about the validity of such classifications and have generally abandoned them on the grounds that they have little or no scientific relevance. The notion of a 'pure' race is a figment of the imagination and most genetic inheritance is shared in common by all the major population groups that have been socially defined as 'races'. The only exceptions to this are a few, essentially trivial, characteristics such as skin colour and certain aspects of physical appearance. There is no evidence to link 'race'-specific genes to any particular economic or political system, or to any level of cultural or social achievement. This is not to say, however, that all scholars have avoided the use of racial categorization in their work. Some, particularly educational and social psychologists such as Arthur Jensen and Hans Eysenck, have argued that measured 'intelligence', by which they mean IQ scores, is consistently higher for samples of 'whites' than for 'blacks' of a similar social composition (Jensen, 1969). Such findings, and the correct interpretation to place upon them, have been the subject of heated debate on both methodological and ideological grounds, the two in this case being closely linked together.

In general, sociologists have tended to favour explanations of an environmental rather than a genetic kind, and have therefore been exceptionally hostile to these theories. They have objected to Jensen's conclusions on a number of counts: that 'intelligence' is a simple property of the mind which can be measured by means of written tests; that it is possible to 'control' environmental influences which can be cumulative over generations and subtle in their operation; that one can produce truly culture-free tests and create a testing atmosphere which will not bias the results; and that differences in so-called intelligence have any independent causal influence on educational or social achievement (Eckberg, 1979). It is interesting to note that many of those who stress the power of genetic determinism, and the inability of environmental forces to affect these fixed characteristics, are among the strongest advocates of separate institutional facilities for groups of different 'abilities'. The paradox between the hereditarian diagnosis and the environmental remedy seems to escape them.

However, most sociologists are not so much concerned with these debates between nature and nurture, or with the truth of biological assertions about the consequences of 'race', but are far more interested in the fact that people really do categorize individuals into such collective units. That the subject under study may be based on outmoded concepts, spurious pseudo-science, or simply be a figment of the imagination, does not matter as far as social relationships are concerned. As W. I. Thomas, one of the founding fathers of the Chicago School of sociology, emphasized in a famous statement: 'If men define situations as real, they *are* real in their consequences.' Anyone doubting the wisdom of this maxim need only consider the part played by rumour in the spread of race riots (Smelser, 1963; Bulmer, 1981). A similar point is brilliantly illustrated by Max Frisch in his play *Andorra*, when the hero Andri, who is murdered in an attempt to appease the anti-Semitism of an invading army, turns out, ironically, not to have been Jewish after all.

It is true that some sociologists have had serious reservations about this subjective emphasis in the analysis of race relations, arguing that such a perspective appears to let 'the racist define the sociologist's area of study' (Rex, 1970; Miles, 1984). However, this concern is based on a misconception. Fears of seeming to subscribe to a racist definition of the situation would be about as well founded as assuming that Freud was religious because he wrote *The Future of an Illusion*. As the title suggests, this work is an attempt to demolish the conventional interpretation of religious thought. The real danger – and this is why sociologists who exclusively stress the subjective perspective, such as ethnomethodologists, have produced so few convincing studies in the area of race relations – is that the social construction of reality does not take place in a vacuum. The key problem is to relate individual and group definitions to the power structure and institutions of society, and this I will do throughout the rest of the book.

Another essential point to remember is that racial and ethnic definitions are highly variable, not so much between individuals but more particularly between groups and societies.[6] Any student of the Caribbean or Latin America is fully aware of the differences between perceptions of colour in these countries, as well as the contrast with the type of definitions to be found in North America. The same individuals of mixed ancestry may be considered to be 'white' in Brazil (provided that they are reasonably wealthy), 'coloured' in Barbados, and 'black' in Birmingham, Alabama (Hoetink, 1967; Pitt-Rivers, 1973). Similar variations can be found between British and Dutch colonial policies so that, as van Amersfoort wryly remarks, 'whereas the British always considered themselves so weak that the slightest drop of foreign blood could de-classify their offspring, the Dutch in their colonies followed the opposite rule. They considered themselves so important that any trace of Dutch ancestry (provided it was legal!) was sufficient to classify a child as Dutch' (van Amersfoort, 1982:57). Thus race relations have little to do with any objective characteristics of 'race' *per se* and much to do with relationships between socially defined groups. The problem for the social scientist then becomes centred on the question of why specific sets of attributes are selected as the basis of group categorization.

This was a distinction lost on sociology's founding fathers whose rejection of racial theorizing was partly due to the particular way the discipline developed. Sociology established itself as a separate area of study at the end of the nineteenth century with masters of social thought such as Emile Durkheim (1858–1917) arguing quite specifically that social facts should be explained in terms of other social facts. By this he meant that social structures and social relationships could only be accounted for in social terms. In his most famous illustration of this argument he claimed that variations in suicide rates between different groups or societies must be explained by the social characteristics of these collective units, and particularly their degree or lack of social cohesion. Explanations that focused on individuals who comprised these groups, whether in terms of their biological nature or their psychological states of mind, Durkheim maintained were irrelevant to an understanding of group dynamics and, therefore, of no interest to the social scientist. It is hardly surprising that followers of the Durkheimian tradition rejected any analysis based on what they regarded as biological 'reductionism', and gave short shrift to the misguided racial theories of their contemporaries.[7]

In a similar manner, but for rather different reasons, Marx's emphasis on the economic determination of social life was clearly hostile to any theory of society based on a racial dynamic. Racial, ethnic and national sentiments could be interpreted either as an outmoded legacy of a previous historical era, destined to be destroyed by the successive onset of the bourgeois and socialist revolutions, or as 'false consciousness', generated by the capitalist class as a means of driving a wedge between sections of the proletariat. In both cases economic factors were paramount and racist ideas became simply reflections of the material base of society. So for Marx, like Durkheim, racial and ethnic groups and racist ideas played a relatively minor part in his interpretation of society and social change.

It was only in the work of Max Weber, the third major architect of modern sociology, whose ideas have had such a dominating influence on our understanding of contemporary society, that there is a significant attempt to incorporate race relations into the mainstream of sociological analysis. But for all of Weber's recognition of racial and ethnic groups as particular kinds of status groups, and his insistence on the autonomous role of ideas in social change, thereby allowing us to appreciate the power of racist ideas and their ability under certain circumstances to take on a life of their own, such contributions are essentially by-products of other themes. It is true that Weber's methodological concern with the interpretative understanding of social action, analysing behaviour in terms of an individual's motives and intentions, ties in with my earlier emphasis on the importance of the 'definition of the situation'. However, despite all these valuable insights, few could reasonably argue that race and ethnicity occupied a particularly central place in his social diagnosis. It was the trend of modern society towards increasing rationality, and the threat of the 'iron cage' of bureaucracy, that preoccupied Weber as the critical problems of his age.

While the classical sociologists were quite correct to dismiss the erroneous racial theories put forward by many of their contemporaries, at times this insistence had the result of throwing out the sociological baby with the biological bathwater. For it led to an underestimation of the extent to which such arbitrary racial definitions might have serious social consequences. Nevertheless, many of the most telling objections to racial theorizing can be found in nineteenth-century debates which are not simply of historical interest since the same basic arguments have been repeated with remarkable regularity over the years. It seems that in this area each generation has to learn anew the lessons of their intellectual forefathers. A good illustration of this can be seen in the classic argument about the respective causal influence of environment and heredity. This has re-emerged in the recent IQ controversies, but its antecedents can be traced back to at least the middle of the last century.

The most influential racial application of this argument can be found in Arthur de Gobineau's notorious *Essay on the Inequality of the Human Races* published in the early 1850s. Although his writings are often confused and contradictory, those aspects of his thought that tried to explain the rise and fall of civilizations in terms of racial mixture and, above all, the central place of the Aryan populations in this process, have earned him the title of 'The Father of Racist Ideology' (Biddiss, 1970). Certain passages of the book provided ideal ammunition for those wishing to assert the claims of white supremacy: 'Such is the lesson of history . . . it shows us that all civilizations derive from the white race, that none can exist without its help, and that a society is great and brilliant only so far as it preserves the blood of the noble group that created it . . .' (Banton, 1977a:43). Gobineau quite specifically ridiculed the argument that racial inequality was the result of customs and institutions. 'We cannot admit', he insisted, 'that the institutions thus invented and moulded by a race of men make that race what it is. They are effects, not causes.' He then proceeded to attack 'the liberal dogma of human brotherhood' which he claimed was denied by the fact that 'the idea of an original, clear-cut, and permanent inequality among the different races is one of the oldest and most widely held opinions in the world' (Stone, 1977:10–13).

In reply to these arguments, Alexis de Tocqueville, the famous author of *Democracy in America* and a life-long personal friend of Gobineau, rejected racial theories on several grounds. First of all, he provided a totally different historical interpretation of the widespread belief in racial superiority. Such attitudes reflected differences in power and the need to rationalize domination and exploitation by means of theories which purported to show that such relationships were inevitable and impossible to change. A closer investigation of the thesis revealed how it was historically naive, for this type of assertion had been repeated throughout the centuries, first by one group and then by another. 'I am sure that Julius Caesar, if he had had the time, would have willingly written a book to show that the savages he met in Britain were not of the same human race as the Romans, and that while the latter were destined by nature to dominate the world, the former were fated to vegetate in an obscure corner' (Stone & Mennell, 1980:321). Thus so much of Gobineau's argument was based on inadequate data and a selective interpretation of history. Tocqueville accepted that there were certain differences between groups but insisted that these were the result of 'thousands of different causes' and not a predestined biological pattern imposed on certain men by reason of race. Finally, Tocqueville went on to stress the social and political consequences of Gobineau's theories: how they had been eagerly and selectively taken up by writers in the Southern states of America who wished to justify slavery, and how his doctrine would inevitably lead to 'all the evils of permanent inborn inequality: pride, violence, contempt for one's fellow men, tyranny and violence in all its forms'.

A similar type of argument reappeared in a slightly different form at the turn of the century when eugenicists such as Francis Galton claimed that it was possible to demonstrate the importance of heredity by tracing the way in which genius could be seen to run in families. Durkheim's reply to this proposition was clear for, like Tocqueville, he firmly rejected any explanation based on innate biological determinants. 'No social phenomenon is known', he declared in his *Rules of Sociological Method*, 'which can be placed in indisputable dependence on race. No doubt we cannot attribute to this proposition the value of a principle; we can merely affirm it invariably true in practical experience' (Durkheim, 1964a:108). In response to Galton's specific claims of inherited genius based on 'veritable dynasties of scholars, poets and musicians' he proposed an alternative hypothesis that explained this concentration as a result of 'family, fortune and education'. He also hinted at the modification of natural selection during the process of social evolution, so that as society became more complex, 'civilization . . . becomes less and less an organic thing, more and more a social thing' (Durkheim, 1964b:321). Thus Durkheim set out a strong argument in favour of environmental rather than hereditary explanations of social life and established a tradition that was to form the mainstream of sociological analysis in the twentieth century.

There have been notable exceptions to this anti-racist bias in the social sciences. The development of sociology and the analysis of race relations by social scientists followed a somewhat different pattern in North America from that in Europe. At the time that Gobineau was writing his *Essay*, Southern 'sociologists' such as Henry Hughes and George Fitzhugh were little more than apologists for the slave system. Not only did they defend slavery as the basis of a moral and civilized society but, following a consistent logic, they also attacked the very notion of democracy itself (Frazier, 1947:265). It is not surprising that Tocqueville, the champion of liberal democracy, should have been concerned about the ready adoption of Gobineau's ideas in the South, although doctrines of racial superiority were closely rooted in the structure of Southern society and hardly needed imported ideologies to add credence to what the typical white slave-owner regarded as self-evident. Intellectual arguments supporting the subordination of blacks were by no means confined to Southern-based sociologists. Many academics in the North East and Mid West fell under the spell of William Graham Sumner of Yale whose social-Darwinism and concept of 'folkways' added a fatalistic determinism to those who supported the existing racial hierarchy. Sumner may not have been a 'racist' in the strict definition of that term but there can be little doubt about the consequences of his theories for race relations (Ball, Simpson & Ikeda, 1962).

Few would dispute Frazier's assessment that in the first two decades of the twentieth century most American sociological theories implicit in the writings on the 'Negro problem' were merely rationalizations of the existing race situation. It is true that prominent pioneering sociologists such as Charles Cooley and Lester Ward were beginning to attack the widespread assumptions about racial types: the former pointing to the empirical inadequacies of Galton's theories because of the impossibility of making meaningful comparisons between blacks and whites who lived under totally different environmental conditions. The real breakthrough in the sociological study of American race relations must be associated with the rise of the Chicago School and is signalled by such influential studies as Thomas and Znaniecki's *Polish Peasant in Europe and America* (1918–20) and Park and Burgess's seminal text-book, *Introduction to the Science of Sociology* (1921). At last an approach to the sociology of race relations was being established which, for all its shortcomings, was conceptualizing race and ethnicity in terms of general sociological processes and not as a consequence of erroneous typological distinctions. Park's famous cycle of race relations consisting of successive phases of group competition, conflict, accommodation and assimilation clearly represents a crude and rather naive analysis of the immigrant experience in America based on an interpretation of European migration into Chicago.[8] Much the same problem is associated with Burgess's model of 'zonal growth' which presents a spatial elaboration of this approach, for neither version can adequately account for the extent and persistence of discrimination against blacks, or for the uneven and irregular patterns of racial and ethnic conflict.

However, despite these problems that are glaringly apparent with the benefit of hindsight, the full measure of the basic change in perspective can be gauged by considering the response to an influential article that appeared, during 1908, in the *American Journal of Sociology*, which was founded and based on the sociology department at Chicago. Written by a Southern sociologist, Alfred H. Stone, its title posed the vital question: 'Is Race Friction between Blacks and Whites in the United States Growing and Inevitable?' The author emphasized what he considered to be the innate 'racial antipathy' between the two groups which was perhaps not a surprising conclusion from someone with a Southern planter pedigree. Of the critical analysis of Stone's thesis only one discussant challenged the twin concepts of racial antipathy and white superiority, and that predictably was the great black sociologist W. E. B. Du Bois. All the other white sociologists writing in the journal continued to discuss these issues in terms of the mental limitations of blacks and the 'natural' repugnance felt between members of the white and 'dark races'.

By the end of the First World War, these assumptions were beginning to lose academic credibility and the gradual increase in the influence of the Chicago School during the 1920s gave added impetus to this trend. After the 1919 race riots in Chicago, one of the first in what was to become a long line of riot commission reports was published under the title *The Negro in Chicago* (1922). This report was largely written by Charles S. Johnson, at that time a young graduate student working under Robert Ezra Park, and it assumed that all racial groups had the same capacity to survive and operate in an urban industrial environment. Pointing to the crucial change in approach, Martin Bulmer remarks:

On several topics – education, crime, industry and the press – the line of analysis tended to start with claims made about black inferiority, show that these claims were considered exaggerated and then argue that what inequality existed was due to social and economic differences, not inherent racial differences. A further assumption of the Commission was that there was no 'natural' hostility between white and black. Tensions which arose were due to social pressures and institutional forms of discrimination and prejudice. (1981:30–1)

From this time onwards American social science increasingly discarded the legacy of racism and turned its attention towards social structural and cultural variables as the major explanatory factors in the analysis of race relations.

A series of important studies were completed on race relations in the South as well as on racial and ethnic patterns in the Northern cities. John Dollard's *Caste and Class in a Southern Town* (1937) was one of the best examples of the first type of study and it emphasized the economic, sexual and status gains that the whites derived from the system of racial domination. The investigations in the Northern cities initiated by Park, Johnson, Wirth and the other Chicago sociologists also represented this new style of social research but covered a greater diversity of racial and ethnic contact situations and relationships. They were concerned with the structure and functioning of systems of racial and ethnic stratification and were based on detailed empirical studies in marked contrast to the armchair theorizing that characterized the writings on this topic in the early years of the century. Together these studies produced a wide range of findings and a set of more systematic theoretical propositions that were to be synthesized, at the end of the Second World War, in Gunnar Myrdal's classic book, *An American Dilemma: The Negro Problem and Modern Democracy* (1944).

While American social science was successfully struggling to emancipate itself from racist forms of explanation, Europe fell increasingly under the sway of fascism. However, no social scientist of any importance succumbed to fascist-inspired racial doctrines and they made very little impact, apart from a negative reaction, on the development of European social thought. Even Vilfredo Pareto (1848–1923), the Italian economist and sociologist who received a measure of favourable attention from Mussolini during his early rise to power, was totally contemptuous of all forms of racist thinking. The Italian dictator may have been impressed by his Machiavellian theory of elites when he launched his imperialist adventures against Abyssinia, but he certainly could not have appreciated the real message of Pareto's major sociological study, *The Treatise on General Sociology* (1916). For the *Treatise* is centrally concerned with exposing the rationalizations employed by individuals and groups in an attempt to justify particular forms of social domination and exploitation. In the work he developed what later social scientists would call a 'power analysis' of race relations (Blalock, 1967; Baker, 1978). This is clearly illustrated in the following passage, taken from an earlier study of socialism, that considers the question of imperialism in Pareto's characteristically uncompromising terms:

There is not perhaps on this globe a single foot of ground which has not been conquered by the sword at some time or other, and where the people occupying it have not maintained themselves on it by force. If the Negroes were stronger than the Europeans, Europe would be partitioned by the Negroes and not Africa by the Europeans. The 'right' claimed by people who bestow on themselves the title of 'civilized' to conquer other peoples whom it pleases them to call 'uncivilized', is altogether ridiculous, or rather, this right is nothing other than force. For as long as the Europeans are stronger than the Chinese, they will impose their will on them; but if the Chinese should become stronger than Europeans, then the roles would be reversed . . . (Finer, 1966:136)

By the outbreak of the Second World War, most sociological theories developed to account for the problems of race relations fully appreciated the divorce between the biological and social concepts of race. The war itself was to accelerate this recognition at a more popular level: partly by its exposure of the vile consequences of Nazi racial doctrines during the Nuremberg trials, and partly by weakening the grip of European colonial powers on their overseas possessions. The 'demonstration effect' of Japanese troops defeating the British army in the Far East did more to undermine the myth of an imperial master race than any amount of nationalist agitation. Furthermore, the use of black soldiers by the United States, in what was declared to be a war against racism, was bound to have some impact on the American black community after the ending of hostilities.

In the immediate postwar era the study of race relations, as indeed the study of sociology in general, was dominated by American scholars, as well as by those exiled Europeans who had settled in North America during the years leading up to the outbreak of the war. There was, however, quite a range of perspectives and a diversity of opinions about what factors were the most important in explaining the dynamics of racial interaction and conflict. Some studies, the most influential of these being *The Authoritarian Personality* (1950) written by Theodor Adorno and his colleagues, focused on the psychopathology of prejudice and argued that a particular type of personality, developed from rigid childrearing practices, often produced a sympathy towards 'fascist' political and social beliefs.[9] In particular, it resulted in hostility directed against blacks, Jews, Catholics and other minorities. This concern with attitudes was one of the dominant preoccupations of American race relations research during the 1950s and was later criticized for underestimating the crucial institutional pressures that cause individuals to discriminate no matter what their personality structure or their beliefs concerning race relations happened to be.

It was this analytical separation between prejudice as an attitude and discrimination as a type of behaviour that provided one important criticism of the second major approach to race relations in the immediate postwar period (Merton, 1949). In *An American Dilemma* Myrdal certainly did not ignore the institutional component of American racial discrimination, but his final interpretation suggested that the underlying dynamic of the system was provided by a major contradiction between theory and practice. This consisted of a conflict between the universalistic values of what he called the 'American Creed' – the doctrine, enshrined in the Constitution and Bill of Rights, that all Americans were entitled to equality before the law regardless of colour, religious beliefs or national origins – and the discriminatory practices that were the norm in everyday contacts between blacks and whites. Despite some early perceptive criticisms from the prominent structural-functionalist sociologist Robert K. Merton and the Marxist scholar Oliver Cromwell Cox, Myrdal's conclusion that this moral tension would eventually force white Americans to dismantle segregation and concede full citizenship rights to blacks was regarded, for almost fifteen years, as the classic diagnosis of the American racial situation. It was only in the late 1950s and early 1960s that articles began to appear subjecting the notion of a value conflict to closer empirical scrutiny. These showed that Myrdal's dilemma was something that most white Americans could either ignore or rationalize without too much discomfort, and that they were certainly reluctant to pay a heavy material price for its resolution. By this time, however, a new generation of black activists and scholars had arrived on the scene who were not prepared to define black oppression as a 'white problem' to be resolved on 'white' terms alone, and with them a whole new phase of American race relations was ushered in.

The third distinctive perspective on race relations in the early postwar period is exemplified by Oliver Cox's *Caste,*

Class and Race (1948), a work that falls within the broad Marxist tradition, although its precise Marxist status has been the subject of some debate (Miles, 1980:169–70). Cox argued that racial categorization and conflict were a direct product of the development of capitalism, for racial oppression was only a special form of the way in which the ruling political class exploited the working classes as a whole. But his predictions about the future development of American race relations derived from this analysis have proved to be as inadequate as those of Myrdal, for he believed that advanced capitalist organization would foster working-class solidarity across racial lines. The 'correct' strategy for blacks, therefore, would be to follow the leadership of 'progressive' whites in a general proletarian struggle. This approach not only exaggerated the revolutionary potential of the class struggle in postwar America but totally failed to come to grips with the crucial problem of working-class racialism.

These three perspectives, seen in the work of Adorno, Myrdal and Cox, shared one point in common: whatever else race relations were about, they had nothing directly to do with biology. It was this assumption, a working out of the classical tradition in sociology, that is perhaps the most characteristic feature of the postwar sociological analysis of race relations, and yet I have already alluded to one set of problems where the older notions of racial typology were far from extinct. The continued use and indeed growth of educational testing procedures, particularly in relation to measuring 'intelligence', has been an enduring feature of Anglo-American social institutions since the early years of the century. Such apparently 'scientific' techniques have been used to justify all manner of social and political policies – from sterilizing 'idiots' to classifying black schoolchildren .as 'educationally subnormal' (Kamin, 1977; Tomlinson, 1981) – and one of the direct consequences has been to keep alive the idea that racial groups have different levels of ability based on genetic inheritance.

Attempts to apportion the relative weight of innate as opposed to acquired skills, in what is clearly a complex interactive relationship, have been pursued with tireless energy and, in the case of Sir Cyril Burt, one of the most influential pioneers in the field, to the point of fraudulently fabricating his evidence. The tenacity with which these scholars have held to their belief in genetic structuring rather than cultural conditioning, and have rejected the claims of bias in their procedures (Jensen, 1980; Taylor, 1981), may be a testimony to their scientific curiosity, but other, less politically naive, interpretations are also possible. Sociologists, particularly since the publication of Thomas Kuhn's influential book *The Structure of Scientific Revolutions* (1962), have tended to be cautious about the claims of 'pure' science; while politicians, notably supporters of racist political parties, have not been slow to seize upon such findings and to employ them for their own ends.[10] It seems that Tocqueville's prophetic warning to Gobineau about the misuse of scholarship for political purposes is just as relevant today as it was in the middle of the nineteenth century.

The IQ controversy is only one area that has called into question the dominant postwar consensus in the social scientific study of race relations. There have been other, newer developments, on the periphery of mainstream sociology, that have had the tendency of resurrecting the notion of an important biological component to social relationships, or, in Pierre van den Berghe's succinct phrase, of 'bringing beasts back in' to sociological analysis (van den Berghe, 1974).[11] One such development has been the rise of sociobiology which, although it has not been centrally focused on issues of race and ethnicity, clearly has important implications for these problems. The conceptual basis of sociobiology grew out of studies of social insects such as ants and bees, and was popularized by E. O. Wilson in his book entitled *Sociobiology: The New Synthesis* (1975). Fundamentally, it is an extension of Darwin's evolutionary theory as applied to animal and particularly human behaviour. Great importance is attached to the mechanism of kin selection as a means of improving individual 'inclusive fitness'. That is to say that in order to preserve their genetic inheritance individuals will cooperate with each other in proportion to the degree to which they are biologically related. Thus human cooperation and apparent 'altruism' can be explained in terms of genetic *selfishness*. A biological basis for ethnocentrism and racism is attributed to an extended version of this process of kin selection which includes not just the family and close relatives, but also tribes, ethnic groups, 'races' and nations. It can then be argued that this also accounts for the 'primordial' attachment to such groups noted by certain scholars writing about race and ethnicity (Shils, 1957; Geertz, 1963).

One of the few explicit applications of this approach to race and ethnic relations can be found in the recent writings of Pierre van den Berghe. This is particularly significant since all his extensive work in the field of comparative race relations, prior to the 1970s, had emphasized conventional sociological variables. Although van den Berghe is careful to state that social relationships among humans are the product not only of kin selection but also of reciprocity and coercion, nevertheless he also makes the claim that a kin-based theory 'accounts for the appearance of racism when and where it does occur better than any competing theory' (van den Berghe, 1978b:407). Thus, in explaining the simultaneous rise of racism and European colonialism he writes:

The colonial expansion of Europe beginning some five centuries ago, and all of the massive population transfers it brought in its wake are, of course, the overwhelmingly important genetic event of our species. Predictably, it brought about a great surge in racism because, all of a sudden, it became possible to make a fairly accurate kin selection judgment from a distance of several hundred meters. The Dutchman at the Cape, the Portuguese in Brazil, the Englishman in Kenya did not have to ask questions and pick up subtle clues of accent to detect kin relatedness. By using a simple test of skin pigmentation he could literally shoot and ask questions later at little risk of killing a kinsman. (ibid)

A peculiar inconsistency appears in the argument, however, for van den Berghe firmly adheres to the view that 'race' is a social construct, while at the same time maintaining that racism is essentially kin-based or biological. The social anthropologist Marshall Sahlins has given many examples of societies where kinship is as much a cultural as a biological phenomenon in his general critique of sociobiology (Sahlins, 1976), while the physical anthropologist Vernon Reynolds argues that biological factors should be seen as constraints on, rather than determinants of social action (Reynolds, 1980:312–15). If kin selection is the prime biological underpinning of race relations, it seems difficult to explain why miscegenation on the slave plantation – to cite an example that van den Berghe discusses in detail (van den Berghe, 1981:111–36) – should take place at all, for it certainly has no simple rationale in sociobiological terms.[12] It may be premature to dismiss sociobiology as 'racist, reductionist and ridiculous' (in the words of its more impatient critics) and the much more measured criticisms of Reynolds might be regarded as a better reflection of our knowledge in this complex interdisciplinary area. But the dangers of this approach are obvious since if racial and ethnic conflicts are struggles between 'primordial' or kin-based groups, then their resolution is a matter of genetic engineering rather than political or economic negotiation. The consequence of such a diagnosis would seem to imply a profound pessimism, if not an outright fatalism, about the future of race and ethnic relations.

Nineteenth- and twentieth-century sociology has attempted to exorcize the biological ghost from the social machine, and the extent to which it has largely succeeded in doing this will become apparent in the lack of biological references found in the chapters that follow. Insofar as it is now possible to discuss virtually every important question in this field without reference to biological evidence, the paradox of race relations without races has been resolved.

2 Minority groups and power

Having established that race relations are not concerned with biological 'races', what do sociologists study when they look at this field? In order to answer this question, I will be considering the following issues: firstly, whether the characteristics which are used to distinguish between groups make any difference to the nature and type of intergroup relationships; whether conflicts and divisions between racially defined groups are fundamentally distinct from those found between ethnic groups; where the boundaries are drawn on the basis of religion, language or national origins. Are differences in colour, and other types of visible distinctions, important elements in intergroup conflict, or are they irrelevant features of the situation, products of historical accidents that have given rise to an illusion which Donald Horowitz has aptly called 'the figment of pigment'?[1] I will then consider the concept of a minority group and show how its definition illustrates the central role of power differences in shaping the various forms of intergroup relations. Finally, I will compare and contrast three models of race relations which all stress certain aspects of differences in power, arising out of slavery, migration, conquest, imperialism or capitalism, and which help to reveal the factors behind the formation and changing conditions of minority groups in society.

Social scientists interested in race relations are concerned with certain forms of group interaction that are *defined* in either racial or ethnic terms. Who 'constructs' these definitions, whether racial or ethnic groups are self-defined or defined by outsiders, and why ethnic or racial criteria are chosen, rather than some other individual or group character-istics, are vitally important considerations. Some sociologists draw a sharp distinction between racial groups, those marked out as biological categories, and ethnic groups, which are defined by a much wider range of cultural, linguistic, religious and national characteristics. The justification for this division is that racial groups are based on immutable, physical attri-butes which are fixed at birth, while ethnic boundaries consti-tute a more flexible form of group differentiation. In certain situations there may be some point in making this distinction for, although 'race' is a social concept with little or no biologi-cal substance, it could be argued that the existence of highly visible markers separating the boundaries between groups adds something qualitatively different to the experience of interracial contacts. In reality, however, there are enough exceptions to this rule to cast serious doubt on any such simple generalization and, in the final analysis, if a difference does exist it is one of degree rather than of kind.

More precisely, there are several reasons why a rigid dis-tinction between racial and ethnic groupings can be positively misleading. In the first place, racial and ethnic characteristics often overlap in any one group, so that individuals who are defined as being members of a particular racial group fre-quently share distinctive languages or dialects, believe in re-ligions or sects that differ from other groups in the society, and possess further unique historical and cultural traditions. It then becomes difficult to separate the 'racial' factor – usually indicated by visible differences in appearance – from the other ethnic and cultural dimensions which determine the strength of the boundaries between groups.[2]

A second problem arises in those societies, which are partic-ularly common in the Caribbean and in Central and South America, where physical appearance is but one of several criteria used in determining an individual's status, so that visual identification is only a very approximate predictor of group membership (Pitt-Rivers, 1973; Dow, 1982). And, thirdly, extremely deep divisions are often found between groups whose visible differences are so imperceptible that they have to be marked out in order to be readily identified. What has been called Japan's 'invisible race', the Burakumin, is an interesting example of a despised minority group which was based historically on certain pariah occupations and whose present members can often only be detected after elaborate investigations.

The fate of the Jews in Nazi Germany is another illustration of the fact that difficulties in identification are in no way related to the severity of discrimination suffered by a persecuted minority group. Before the Nazis came to power in 1933, Jews had been more closely integrated into the mainstream of German society than in most other European countries and few Germans seriously questioned their loyalty to the state during the First World War. After the Nazi takeover, however, strenuous efforts had to be made to identify and distinguish Jews from the rest of society in order to pursue increasingly anti-Semitic policies which culminated in the genocidal massacre of the 'final solution'.

Some of the clearest evidence that visibility in itself is neither a necessary nor a sufficient factor in determining the level and intensity of intergroup conflict can be seen in the different treatment accorded to various individuals and groups under the system of apartheid in South Africa. For example, the Japanese and Chinese are granted different status, as are African diplomats and visiting black celebrities, in contrast to local Africans or migrant labourers. In the first case, both the Japanese and Chinese are readily identifiable as 'non-white', although some whites find it difficult to distinguish between the two, and yet the Japanese have been accepted as 'honorary whites' while the Chinese are classified as a distinct and subordinate group. This means that the Chinese are assigned to separate and unequal facilities in such important spheres as employment, housing, education and welfare, while the Japanese share all the privileges of the dominant white group.

The reason behind this apparently arbitrary distinction – reminiscent of Nazi Germany's definition of their Japanese allies as 'honorary Aryans' – can be found in the strategic value of Japan's trade and investment to South Africa. Against a background of mounting pressure for economic sanctions and boycotts aimed at bringing about the end of apartheid, the Nationalist government has turned a blind eye to the many inconsistencies in its racial policies. Another element in this case is that the Japanese, who make up a tiny, transient business and diplomatic community, are unlike the Chinese, who have lived in small numbers in the country since they were introduced as indentured labourers to work in the gold mines at the turn of the century. The Japanese have never formed a permanent community within South African society. As a result, their acceptance by the dominant white group does not pose any threat to the established racial hierarchy and can be rationalized as a pragmatic measure, like the concessions granted to foreign black diplomats and sportsmen, to counter South Africa's increasing isolation from the rest of the world.

These anomalies force the attention of the student of race relations away from a consideration of the visibility of a particular group, or even its cultural characteristics, for the only way to account for such striking differences in treatment is in terms of variations in the economic, political and social balance of power. This approach has similarities to that proposed by certain anthropologists who have stressed the importance of boundary mechanisms and situational structures, rather than the content of supposedly 'fixed' cultures, as the proper subject matter of race and ethnic relations (Barth, 1969:198–9; Okamura, 1981:452–65).

A further illustration that it is differences in *power*, and the dynamic change of power resources over time, that provide the key to an understanding of racial and ethnic conflict can be seen by comparing two types of group violence in Britain. Some observers have argued that parallels drawn between the hostility of the Catholic and the Protestant communities in Northern Ireland, which is usually described as a 'religious' or nationalist conflict, and the racial violence in the urban areas of the mainland, are misleading. It is true that the sectarian gunman who enters a public house in Belfast and demands to know the religion of the drinkers before deciding who to murder has an identification problem not faced by the white racialist intent on attacking blacks in the streets of Brixton or Bradford. However, apart from this immediate contrast, the similarities in the two situations are more instructive than the differences. Both incidents of violence take place against a background of differential group power, perpetuated over the years in customary patterns of social relations and institutions, and both are to some degree a legacy of colonialism. In the one case, Protestants drawn originally from England and Scotland colonized the Catholic Irish over a period of several hundred years; in the other, former colonial subjects moved to the metropolitan society to take up employment at the bottom of the economic ladder in jobs generally shunned by the local white working classes.

As a result of these shared experiences, there have emerged clearly defined groups stratified in terms of political power, social status and economic rewards. Each group lives in predominantly separate neighbourhoods, is educated in largely different schools, and tends to marry within their own group (Barritt & Carter, 1972; Rose, 1969). Without strong countervailing pressures from outside the main arena of conflict, little change in these patterns of domination is likely. In Northern Ireland, external forces have tended to promote, rather than reduce, the level of violence, while in the rest of Britain successive governments have pursued anti-discrimination policies with less than full commitment so that these measures have proved to be a slow and ineffectual remedy for institutionalized racial disadvantage. Even during periods of apparent quiescence the ingredients for intercommunal tension have remained dormant, needing only a minor provocation to spark off sectarian or racial violence (Scarman, 1981).

While physical appearance might then seem to be an unimportant element in race and ethnic relations, it is nevertheless undeniable that group boundaries cannot be enforced without the ability to distinguish effectively between groups. For example, when the Nationalist government came to power in South Africa in 1948 one of its initial measures taken to establish apartheid, a policy of legalized racial segregation, was concerned with defining 'racial' groups for administrative purposes (van den Berghe, 1965:85). The Population Registration Act (1950) was the first of a series of new laws designed to enforce rigid group membership by attempting to define who belonged to each officially labelled, 'racial' group. This was no easy task in a society where racial mixing had proceeded for several centuries producing an intermediate Coloured group which numbered more than one million people at the time the legislation was passed.[3] It is of particular interest that the criterion used for this purpose was not simply physical appearance, those who looked as though they were members of a particular group, but social repute, those who had been customarily regarded as members of a given community. In this way, a political philosophy built on assertions about racial difference conceded that social definitions, in the last resort, were more crucial than physical characteristics.

There are occasions, however, when considering racial and ethnic conflicts as essentially similar can appear to cause confusion, but this is usually the result of equating circumstances that are in other important respects quite different. A good example of this can be seen in the controversial analogies drawn between white immigrant groups in the United States and the situation of American blacks. It is not that racial, as opposed to ethnic, markers are so vital, as the remarkable economic success of the Japanese in postwar America testifies (Bonacich & Modell, 1980), but rather that the historical and social variables involved in each case are not identical (Lieberson, 1980). The linking of these groups, with the implication that their economic, social and political experiences are comparable, can be dangerously (and some would claim deliberately) misleading.

Historians and sociologists have pointed out the obvious, as well as the more subtle, differences between the life experiences of the Southern black moving to the industrial cities of the North, as compared to those of the European immigrant residing in New York, Philadelphia, Washington or Chicago. The European immigrant arrived during a period of rapid urban-industrial expansion when there was a strong demand for unskilled labour. Large families meant that there were many income earners in each household, even if they were paid at abysmally low wages, so increasing the total family income and the possibility of saving. Even the ethnic cultures and an inability to speak English had the unanticipated advantage of promoting ethnic service industries, thereby nurturing small-scale entrepreneurial activities. Furthermore, the European immigrant did not have to face racial discrimination and, being white, could even push blacks out of the few occupations in which they had established themselves in the cities.

When Southern blacks came North, not as 'immigrants' at all but as former slaves of several generations standing, they faced an already developed industrial economy with a declining demand for unskilled labour. The power of the political machines was waning and the spoils and patronage that remained were already monopolized by white immigrants and their children, who did not hesitate to practise racial discrimination in order to avoid any black encroachments on their hard-earned privileges. Of course, it would be wrong to argue that there were no similarities between the situation of blacks and white immigrants. Indeed, writing in the late 1960s, Herbert Gans commented:

Family breakdown, desertion, alcoholism, and all the other forms of social and individual pathology rampant in the ghetto today were equally prevalent in the slums of the early twentieth century. Moreover, white Americans tend to overestimate the speed with which their ancestors escaped from poverty in comparison with Negroes. The fact is that among the various ethnic groups who came to America in the last big waves of immigration, only the Jews, who were already urbanized, have totally escaped poverty. The Italians, Poles, Greeks, Slovenians – and even the Irish – who, like the Negroes, came to America with peasant backgrounds, are only now, after three generations, in the final stages of that escape . . . in short, it took these ethnic groups three and sometimes four generations to achieve the kind of middle-class income and status that means affluence in today's America. Negroes have been in the city for only two generations, and they have come under much less favorable conditions. (1968 in 1977:203–4)

The practical consequence of ignoring these differences is to imply that the same methods are appropriate for securing black progress towards 'full citizenship' in American society as have been used by the white ethnic groups. However, the problems faced by blacks, and their continued exclusion from participation in many areas of American society (Roof, 1978:461–2), emphasize the danger of superficial analogies. There can be little doubt that one group can learn from the experiences of another and some scholars, such as Ali Mazrui, have argued that American blacks might usefully develop a black consciousness on the model of the Jewish Talmudic tradition: 'a black Talmudic tradition is needed – at once different in content from its Jewish counterpart and comparable in function at the same time' (Mazrui, 1978:19–35). However, this does not mean that black and Jewish experiences in America are similar and to suggest that they are can be quite misleading.

The fierce arguments over the use of quotas in education or employment is a clear indication of this point. There was considerable tension in the late 1960s in the New York public school system, with its high percentage of Jewish teachers and an equally high black student enrolment, over such issues as the 'community control' of education. A major reason for the objection to quotas was because this device was used to discriminate against well-qualified and highly motivated Jewish students in the first half of the twentieth century and became a hated symbol of anti-Semitism. On the other hand, blacks coming from circumstances of educational deprivation not offset by a domestic and community environment capable of compensating for formal disadvantage might indeed need a guaranteed *minimum* of places as a means of obtaining a fairer proportion of educational resources. Few would be naive enough to expect that reserving a quota would be a sufficient measure for creating equality of opportunities – still less equality of results – but it might be a necessary stage in a long-term move in that direction. In this way, the contro-versial issue of 'positive discrimination' (which I will discuss in greater detail in the final chapter) became a wedge between many black and Jewish leaders who had formerly been allies in the battle against all forms of discrimination (Goren, 1980:594).

While racial and ethnic groups may be distinguished by whether the boundary is marked out in physical or cultural terms, some would argue that the concept of a 'minority' is a better tool to use in the analysis of race and ethnic relations. The term 'minority' avoids some of the definitional problems discussed above, particularly those concerned with the nature and significance of different types of group markers, and focuses attention on the size and strength of the groups in-volved, which are far more important characteristics in the determination of group behaviour and relationships. Nevertheless, the use of minority groups as a basic unit of analysis raises other questions that need to be clarified. Most sociologists start with Louis Wirth's classic definition of a minority as a 'group of people distinguished by physical or cultural characteristics subject to different and unequal treat-ment by the society in which they live and who regard them-selves as victims of collective discrimination' (Wirth, 1945:347).

Wirth emphasizes three basic elements. Firstly, the *cultural and/or physical markers* of the group that set out its boundaries. These I have discussed in the earlier parts of this chapter. A second element in Wirth's definition is the fact that a minority is subject to *collective discrimination*, and is thereby placed in a subordinate structural position in society. This emphasizes the power dimension of the situation and links the study of race and ethnic relations to what sociologists call social stratifica-tion, the unequal distribution of economic, social and political resources within society (Blalock, 1960; 1982; Rex, 1970; 1981). The third part of Wirth's definition deals with the *subjective consciousness* and *identification* of minority group members. As in the case of class analysis, this is extremely important particularly when considering the political conflicts generated between minority and majority groups. Unless individuals regard themselves as members of the same minority, sharing both ethnic awareness and ethnic consciousness (McKay & Lewins, 1978; Cross, 1978:38–44), they are unlikely to act together to fight for group rights or to strive to protect group interests. Just as Marx's analysis of capitalist society depended, to an important degree, on the extent to which a class-in-itself – one objectively defined in relation to the means of capitalist production – would become self-conscious as a revolutionary class-for-itself, so the dynamic analysis of race relations also depends on the extent to which racial and ethnic groups develop racial and ethnic consciousness. Political mobilization, and hence political action, depends entirely on the development of such a conscious awareness and identification of the individual with the ethnic or racial group.

Whether a minority group has anything to do with actual numbers is an issue that is sometimes raised, but one that is largely a matter of definition. I would hesitate to talk of a 'minority' that is in fact a numerical majority of the population. Wirth does this, as do many sociologists, wishing to emphasize the power rather than the numerical aspect of the definition. The problem with this approach can be seen in contrasting the situation of black Africans in South Africa with the very different circumstances of American blacks. Both groups might be described as minorities if we focus on the power dimension of the concept, even though in one society they make up seventy per cent of the population, while in the other they constitute a group of approximately ten per cent. However, this basic demographic fact will affect many different aspects of race relations, not least the question of the 'costs' for the dominant group of promoting racial justice: whether such policies can be pursued in a relatively peaceful, evolutionary manner, or whether they are more likely to lead to persistent conflict and violence. It is not simply a question of emphasis, since the power and the numerical dimensions of the concept are ultimately linked to each other (van Amersfoort, 1978:218–34).

In fact, van Amersfoort, who provides one of the most systematic evaluations of the term minority group, relates the numerical dimension directly to the question of political power:

The characteristic problem for a minority group in the modern democratic state is not so much that it is difficult to ensure formal rights, but that the numerical situation restricts the possibility of translating such rights into social influence. (ibid, 221)

The intractable issue of protecting minority rights under a system of majority rule is just as formidable a challenge to a modern democracy as the defence of individuals and minorities under autocratic regimes. This is no more than an echo of the fears expressed by Tocqueville in his prophecy that the 'tyranny of the majority' would be one of the inherent dangers facing a mass, democratic society (Stone & Mennell, 1980:99–101). Thus the concept of a minority group must include both the numerical and the power dimensions as recognized by a comparative sociologist such as Richard Schermerhorn who has developed a fourfold typology out of these factors (1970:13). This includes not only *majorities* and *minorities*, dominant and subordinate in terms of both numbers and strength, but also *elites* and *subordinated masses*, where numerical superiority and power do not coincide. However, there are additional dimensions to the concept that need to be considered.

The respective goals of the majority and minority are of great importance. Wirth, for example, emphasized the latter, suggesting that different minorities aim to achieve varying relationships with the rest of society, and that these can be broadly described as pluralism, assimilation, secession and domination (1945:354). But, as van Amersfoort points out, it is wrong to look at minority goals in isolation from the aims of the majority group in society. Any attempt to develop a broad typology, capable of classifying the full range of race and ethnic relations on a cross-national basis, must include both sets of orientations and consider their dynamic interaction.

The attitude of the dominant society towards minorities is unusually important if the assumptions behind a power analysis of race and ethnic relations are accepted. This is because the majority has a disproportionate ability to impose its preferred pattern of relationships on the minority group. As a general rule, it is reasonable to expect that the greater the imbalance of power between majority and minority, the worse will be the disadvantages suffered by the minority. To some degree this may be influenced by the extent to which the minority is located in a particular regional or urban setting, whether it is a *concentrated* or *dispersed* minority (van Amersfoort, 1978:229). Minorities who live in large numbers in inner city areas, or who even form a numerical majority in certain regions, may have greater political, economic or strategic leverage than other minorities scattered more evenly throughout a state. Where democratic electoral systems operate on a 'winner takes all' basis, rather than some form of proportional representation, a concentrated minority vote is likely to be much more effective than a dispersed group's vote (Lee, 1983:213–20). The same may also be true in the industrial sector where a minority's monopoly over a specific occupation, or a vital part of the productive process, can increase its bargaining power. However, under authoritarian systems, or where there is totalitarian rule, such concentration can work in the opposite direction to facilitate the identification, exploitation and even extermination of minority groups.

Just as the minority group will have a range of orientations towards the dominant society which will vary on a continuum from assimilation to secession, so, too, will there be a corresponding set of attitudes among the majority group. In practice, of course, there will rarely be unanimity of goals within either the minority or majority groups, although a dominant viewpoint can generally be isolated. Van Amersfoort summarizes these choices into three major categories, what he terms *emancipation*, *continuation* and *elimination*. Emancipation implies policies aimed at ensuring full citizenship rights for minorities without insisting on either their cultural or structural assimilation. Such a strategy does not necessarily result in the disappearance of the minority group as a distinct community. The goal of continuation seeks to preserve the existing relationship between majority and minority, which may result in continued exploitation but need not necessarily produce this effect. Certain minorities may prefer to be left alone to pursue a symbiotic, if usually unequal, relationship with the dominant society. There are two types of policy that can be described as elimination: on the one hand, the majority may pursue measures aimed at the forced assimilation of the minority, generally involving an assault on its language, religion or culture, in an attempt to eradicate differences and replace them by the traditions of the dominant group. On the other hand, elimination can involve the physical removal of a minority from the state by expulsion, for example the forced exodus of the Asians from Uganda during the dictatorship of Idi Amin (Pereira et al., 1978); or extermination, as in the Nazi holocaust of European Jews or the Turkish genocide against the Armenians.

These various dimensions of the minority concept can be combined to produce a valuable typology of majority–minority relationships which suggests a number of probable outcomes. The interesting conclusion from this exercise is, as van Amersfoort rightly stresses, that 'it demonstrates how rare are the possibilities for a positive development of relationships between majority and minority. Only the cells marked "emancipation process" and "federalism" suggest the prospect of a stable form of minority participation in society' (van Amersfoort, 1978:231). It is for this reason that minority relationships are so often marked by conflict, friction and instability, and why the need to protect minority groups is such a universal and persistent problem throughout the world (Wirsing, 1981).

Having established a more precise understanding of the constituent elements of minority groups and, what is probably

Typology of majority–minority relations

orientation of majority	dispersed minorities orientation		concentrated minorities orientation	
	universalistic	*particularistic*	*universalistic*	*particularistic*
emancipation	emancipation process	sectarian minority	federalism	secessionist movement; eventually secession
continuation	suppression (struggle for emancipation)	reservation situation	suppression (struggle for regional autonomy)	secessionist war
elimination	forced assimilation or extermination	forced assimilation or extermination	forced assimilation or extermination	secessionist war; forced assimilation or extermination

Source: J.M.M. van Amersfoort (1978), 'Minority as a Sociological Concept'. *Ethnic and Racial Studies*, 1,2: 231

of greater importance, the various components of minority group status, the next stage of our analysis is a consideration of more systematic models and typologies of race and ethnic relations. These models provide the social scientist with a simplified set of variables and can enable him to make comparisons between situations of racial conflict and harmony in diverse cultural and historical settings. It should be apparent from my previous argument that a central issue in the comparative sociology of race relations is the manner in which power is distributed among the different groups in society. Few aspects of race relations can be understood without considering the way in which power is exercised throughout society, although it must be recognized that the nature and dynamics of power relationships is an exceedingly complex topic.

In his writings on the subject, Blalock (1967; 1979) has

stressed two major aspects of power: the one element consists of *power resources*, while the other concerns the *mobilization* of these resources. The power resources available to a group comprise their numerical strength which, under a democratic political regime, translates, however approximately, into votes and political representation. They also include the income, wealth and other economic assets possessed by group members, in addition to their education and skills which economists frequently refer to as human capital. More intangible group characteristics, such as social organization, prestige and the authority that it enjoys in a society, should not be overlooked. The mobilization element refers to the more dynamic aspects of resource utilization and includes such factors as group leadership, the motivation of its members, its cohesiveness and its adaptability to changing circumstances. Clearly both the resources available and how they are mobilized are extremely important in determining the relative balance of power between the various groups in society. This power model of race relations can be refined in a number of ways by considering the effects of strategies, alliances and coalitions that may be employed when more than two groups are operating within a given situation (Baker, 1978:317; Stone, 1975:15–18). If, as I have argued, the degree of discrimination and disadvantage suffered by minority groups is closely associated with the extent of the imbalances in power between dominant and subordinate groups, then a set of preliminary questions emerge that any analysis of racial and ethnic conflict must address. For example, Donald Noel recognizes this when he isolates three basic elements, *ethnocentrism*, *competition* and *power*, as the vital ingredients of any general theory of race relations (Noel, 1968:157–72).

It was the failure to incorporate an adequate appreciation of the importance of differences in power that was a major defect of some of the earliest models of race relations developed by sociologists, such as the race relations cycles pioneered by Robert Park and his colleagues in Chicago. This error accounts for their one-sided and, what can be clearly seen in retrospect, highly distorted view of the development of race relations. A similar criticism also applies to the early postwar attempts to interpret British race relations in terms of the so-called 'stranger' hypothesis, a notion quickly abandoned by its proponents as it became obvious that cultural ignorance and misunderstandings, on the part of both black immigrants and the local white population, were only a relatively minor cause of racial conflict and discrimination in Britain from the late 1950s onwards.

In the postwar period, the most useful comparative models of race and ethnicity have been those that have stressed certain aspects of power relations as being particularly crucial to an understanding of the dynamics and development of racial and ethnic interaction. I will select three of the most influential of these: those formulated by Pierre van den Berghe (1978a), Stanley Lieberson (1961) and John Rex (1981) for more detailed discussion. Van den Berghe contrasts the typical pattern of race relations found under plantation slavery and other pre-industrial economic systems with those occurring in industrial settings. Stanley Lieberson's focus is on patterns of migration and conquest and how they affect the subsequent evolution of race relations. While John Rex emphasizes the interplay between colonial and metropolitan stratification that has continued to operate in an increasingly integrated world economic system. In their different ways, all three approaches stress power differentials that arise in various contexts and the implications these have for group relations.

Van den Berghe proposes two ideal types of race relations which he calls the *paternalistic* and the *competitive* patterns. Each corresponds to a set of characteristic relationships so that the paternalistic pattern is generally found in a variety of pre-industrial economic systems, such as mercantile capitalism, slave plantations or in feudal agricultural settings. With the onset of industrialization, this pattern tends to change to a substantially different set of relationships in which active competition between racial and ethnic groups replaces the more settled domination of the paternalistic system. These two patterns mirror that familiar historical transition emphasized by many nineteenth- and early twentieth-century social scientists: what Weber described as the movement from traditional to rational- legal authority and Toënnies the displacement of community (*Gemeinschaft*) by association (*Gesellschaft*). It is this theme that has found its way into subsequent social science literature, expressed in slightly different language but in a basically unaltered form: in anthropology, as Redfield's 'folk-urban continuum', and, in sociology, as the pattern variables discussed by Talcott Parsons.[4]

All these terms represent an attempt to capture the essence of modern society and to differentiate its characteristics from an earlier pre-industrial age. If there is a large measure of agreement about the significance of this transition, it is not surprising that such a major social watershed should be accompanied by equally profound changes in the nature of race and ethnic relations. The key characteristics of the paternalistic pattern can then be contrasted with its competitive counterpart, so providing a set of benchmarks against which to assess major historical changes, as well as to make comparisons between different societies. What then are the major features of each ideal type? In a paternalistic system the division of labour is along racial lines, with the subordinate group performing the heavy manual tasks, particularly those in agriculture, while in the competitive system this castelike monopoly of occupations breaks down. The demands of a complex industrial economy make the maintenance of a rigid colour bar increasingly costly in terms of efficiency; while shared skills in both the dominant and subordinate group result in intense competition for the better rewarded jobs that are no longer the exclusive preserve of the dominant minority. Such competition can be particularly fierce where there are discrepancies between the individual's racial status and level of skills, that is, among the marginal members of both castes, leaving the impoverished and poorly educated upper-caste member feeling enormously insecure, while the better educated or wealthy lower-caste member experiences acute relative deprivation. The poor whites of the American South and the equivalent group in South Africa, the *bywoners*, during the interwar years, are examples of the first category, while many racial revolutionaries and ethnic nationalists have been bred by the second set of circumstances.[5]

There are related differences in a variety of other spheres. Increasing social and geographical mobility found in the competitive type contrasts with the static character of the slave plantation or feudal serfdom. In the cases that van den Berghe emphasizes, the numerical ratios between dominant and subordinate groups change so that the small dominant minority of the paternal system gives way to a dominant majority under competition. There is also a break-up in the traditional value systems with the ideological 'consensus' of the slave plantation or feudalism, characterized by the 'benevolent despotism' of the master and the subservience of the slaves, being replaced by the conflicting values of the competitive system.[6] These value conflicts are usually between the universalistic ideology of the competitive society and the discriminatory practices that are still prevalent, if no longer unchallenged. Elaborate rituals of deference used to symbolize and reinforce racial domination, which have been called the 'etiquette of race relations' (Doyle, 1937), gradually collapse into an undefined set of relationships and codes of interracial behaviour. Spatial segregation becomes a more prominent mechanism to maintain social distance between groups as the chasm separating individuals of different status in an earlier era is increasingly eroded. Interracial sexual relations, which were almost exclusively between upper-caste males and lower-caste females, become extremely rare and invite disapproval from both groups, while the stereotypes held of the lower status groups change from a patronizing contempt to a stronger sense of fear and hatred.

Van den Berghe is careful to emphasize the limits of his typology, to show that 'mixed types' may often be found and that paternal and competitive relationships can coexist within the same society. The rivalry against Jews in medieval Europe was clearly competitive in nature and occurred in those societies whose social relations, in the predominantly rural sectors, closely approximated to the paternal ideal type. Of course, with any such broad attempt to classify an enormous range of variables, specific criticisms and counterexamples can be cited (Mason, 1970:60–3). Nevertheless, the division between paternalistic and competitive patterns does provide some useful insights into the complexity of the relationships between racial and ethnic groups, and helps to capture major features of some of the most significant developments in recent historical times.

A slightly different perspective, with a primary emphasis on migration and conquest, has been proposed by Stanley Lieberson. The transition described by van den Berghe, while in no sense intended as a conventional Marxist analysis, places a stress on the changing nature of the economic base of society, with its ramifications throughout the social and cultural system. Lieberson chooses to pinpoint the initial stages of interracial contact as having a profound impact on the subsequent development of intergroup relations. He takes as his starting point the limitations that I have already noted in Park's race relations cycle and outlines a theory that, he claims, can systematically account for differences between 'societies in such divergent consequences of contact as racial nationalism and warfare, assimilation and fusion, and extinction' (Lieberson, 1961:902). What is crucial in this theory is whether the initial contacts involve the subordination of an indigenous population by a migrant group, or whether such contacts take place in the reverse direction, with the migrant population being subordinated by an indigenous racial or ethnic group. The typical colonial conquest provides examples of the first situation; while the massive migrations into the United States during the nineteenth and early twentieth centuries, or the migrant labour movements into postwar Europe, illustrate the second case. Having developed this major distinction between early forms of contact, Lieberson then traces its implications for the subsequent evolution of race and ethnic relations.

Such a simplified scheme raises a number of basic questions, not the least of which is how to define an 'indigenous' population. Lieberson adopts a working definition which designates as 'indigenous' any group capable of maintaining 'some minimal form of social order' over several generations, rather than a necessarily 'aboriginal' population. This definition, which stresses power relationships rather than historical claims as the crucial criteria, means that it is the white Anglo-Saxon Protestants rather than the American Indians, or white Australians rather than the Aborigines, that are regarded as the *sociologically* indigenous groups. As a result of adopting this perspective, the indigenous group may change over time and the migrant group may, after several generations, take on the characteristics of an indigenous population. It is under these circumstances that intergroup conflict is likely to be particularly intense, as the former migrant group becomes firmly entrenched and there are competing claims as to which group is the legitimate occupier of the land. Savage interracial violence in Algeria and the intractable conflicts in Southern Africa and Northern Ireland illustrate this outcome.

The contrast between the two major types of development is that where the indigenous group is conquered, in the classical colonial pattern, this will produce greater interracial conflict than in situations where migrant groups join a new society in a subordinate position. A typical sequence of events flowing from migrant domination involves the decimation of indigenous peoples, often as much by the introduction of new diseases as by physical extermination. However, genocidal destruction often does take place and depends, in large measure, on disparities in the levels of technology of the groups concerned. The 'frontier' situations in Australia and New Zealand, Southern Africa and North America provide numerous examples of such conflicts (Lamar & Thompson, 1981; Reynolds, 1982). More tightly organized and technologically sophisticated groups, such as the Maoris or the Zulus, were better able to resist genocidal massacres than the Australian Aborigines or the bushmen of South Africa. In addition to a sharp decline in population, there is also a serious disruption, if not a total collapse, of the indigenous economic and political institutions. All these developments reflect the significant levels of intergroup conflict which may appear to decline in the aftermath of conquest, but which tend to re-emerge at a later stage when the migrant group is challenged or over-thrown in a nationalist or anti-colonial liberation struggle. The violence of migrant domination is captured in the writings of Frantz Fanon, particularly in his book *The Wretched of the Earth*, where he interprets it as an inherent part of the coloniz-ing process as well as a necessary part of decolonization.

In contrast, the situation of migrant subordination will pro-duce far less violence and the outcome is more likely to result in a relatively peaceful pluralism, or to lead to the eventual assimilation of the migrant group. There are several reasons that account for this difference: partly, because the migrants have a range of options as to where they can go and, partly, because a strong indigenous group can determine the level and composition of any migrant flows into the country by means of immigration regulations and other legislation. Here Lieberson is considering the typical pattern of European migration into the United States or other major immigrant societies. Without denying that friction does occur in these circumstances, the argument is that it is significantly different from the violence accompanying colonialism.

The scheme can also be developed to consider rather more complex, and hence more realistic, patterns of interethnic and interracial relations that involve more than just two groups. Where there is migrant domination, other ethnic groups may be introduced to work in positions that the indigenous popula-tion are unwilling or unable to fill. Many of the small trading and lesser bureaucratic functions of the European empires were undertaken by Chinese or Indian immigrants specifically recruited by the colonial administrators for these tasks. In the post-colonial era, the nationalist governments of such newly independent states have often taken measures designed to coun-terbalance the commercial advantages that these groups have achieved relative to the indigenous peoples. Some of the reactions have been drastic, with much of the resentment felt against the colonial powers spilling over onto these intermediary groups who were highly visible as shopkeepers, traders and frontline officials. The violence against the Chinese population in post-independence Indonesia, the harassment and expulsion of East African Asians, or the attacks against the Tamils in Sri Lanka are some of the more extreme consequences of this scenario. Other reactions have been more measured, and involve the granting of systematic preference or quotas to favour the politically dominant group in education, government service and employment. In Malaysia, such policies have been used to improve the situation of the *bumiputras* (sons of the soil), which work to the current disadvantage of non-Malays, notably the Chinese and Indians. They are justified as compensatory measures to rectify the imbalances of wealth and general economic opportunities produced by the colonial system (Abraham, 1983; Lim, 1985). These are examples of positive discrimination, operating in the developing world, which I will discuss in greater detail in later chapters.

Multiple ethnic contacts evolve in a somewhat different manner where the indigenous population is in control at the time additional groups arrive in the society. A good illustration of this can be found in Hawaii, where the 'indigenous' population (i.e. whites or *haoles*, rather than native Hawaiians) have manipulated the intake of other ethnic groups by shifting from one source to another in order to prevent any single group from gaining too much power. The great variety of immigrant groups in Hawaii, including Chinese, Japanese, Portuguese, Puerto Ricans, Koreans, Spaniards, Russians and Filipinos, reflects a conscious policy on the part of plantation owners and other major employers to diversify their labour supply, thereby operating a variation on the familiar strategy of divide and rule.[7]

The difference between the two basic models can be summarized in the following terms:

In societies where whites are superordinate but do not settle as an indigenous population, other racial and ethnic groups are admitted in large numbers and largely in accordance with economic needs of the revised economy of the habitat. By contrast, when a dominant migrant group later becomes indigenous, in the sense that the area becomes one of permanent settlement through generations for the group, migrant populations from new racial and ethnic stocks are restricted in number and source. (Lieberson, 1961:907)

As in the case of van den Berghe's distinction between the paternalistic and competitive ideal types, Lieberson's dichotomy seeks to explain complex patterns in terms of a few key variables. This can be useful in attempts to predict the possible development of race and ethnic relations, to understand historical patterns, and to make cross-cultural comparisons. However, many problems arise when analysing specific cases in these terms if they are not used in a flexible and dynamic way. To take one example, South African society clearly exhibits elements of both migrant and indigenous subordination fused in a series of complex relationships (Lever, 1978:81), just as it contains competitive and paternalistic characteristics according to van den Berghe's scheme. It can also be argued that Lieberson's model, while incorporating the element of differential power in a much more realistic manner than Park's race relations cycle, does not provide a clear interpretation of the history of blacks in America. This is because the situation of black Americans represents a very different type of migrant subordination than the later European migrations that did not result in slavery.[8]

Lieberson does not claim that his theory is a comprehensive explanatory model that can account for each and every case of race or ethnic relations. It is perhaps better seen as an attempt to highlight certain important variables that establish the general context in which many other factors operate. The ratio of numbers between groups, the competitive or complementary nature of economic activities, visibility and cultural distinctiveness and prevailing racial ideas will also combine to produce specific outcomes. One further criticism of Lieberson's model might be that it does not establish any clear link between the two basic situations or interpret them as part of an interrelated process. The final example of a race relations paradigm that I will discuss, presented in the writings of John Rex, does make a direct attempt to relate the patterns of race relations operating under these two sets of conditions.

Rex is quite explicit in viewing patterns of race and ethnic relations as part of a general, interconnected system (Rex, 1981:1–25). With regard to contemporary British race relations, he makes the point that 'in a very real sense the slave plantations of the Caribbean in the seventeenth and eighteenth centuries were part of the social structure of modern Britain' (1981:3). In broad terms, this is an attempt to integrate the situation in metropolitan societies, which parallels Lieberson's indigenous superordination and van den Berghe's competitive ideal type, with the circumstances operating in colonial and ex-colonial societies, which exhibit, or have recently passed beyond, the phase of migrant superordination and paternalism. However, this is not simply the uncontroversial assertion that history is an essential part of an understanding of any pattern of race relations, but a much more debatable claim that these situations form part of an international capitalist economy or modern world system, to use the terminology popularized by Immanuel Wallerstein (1974). The uneven development of capitalism has led certain countries and regions of growth – economic 'cores' – to systematically exploit less advanced societies and regions – 'peripheries' – and many types of race and ethnic relations arise from 'the interaction between the centre and the periphery through migration' (Rex, 1981:4). While Wallerstein curiously underplays the importance of empires in his analysis of the development of this system, Rex stresses the imperial factor as a central theme.

There are three major aspects of the colonial social structure that merit particular attention: the pre-colonial social forms, the type of colonial exploitation and the system of social and racial stratification that develops out of the interaction between the first two. It is important to recognize the diversity of pre-colonial societies and cultures since this does influence the evolution of the colonial social structure. The difficulties encountered by colonial conquerors in trying to induce or force the Indians of both North and South America to work as plantation labourers was a major factor in the initiation and expansion of the slave trade, and thereby had a profound impact on subsequent patterns of race relations. Not only can the indigenous social structure affect the type of colonial economy and influence the path of post-colonial development, it may also have a crucial role to play in the lives of those who migrate to metropolitan societies. As Rex comments, 'transported and migrating workers will not be simply so much dust to be blown around by capitalism either in other colonies or in the metropolis itself, but rather men, constituted by their own social and cultural systems and acting accordingly' (1981:8).

Just as there are several types of pre-colonial societies, so there is a considerable range of systems of colonial economic exploitation. There is the trading and plundering found in the early stages of colonial contact, of which the Spanish conquest of South America is probably the supreme example. This is often followed by more permanent forms of exploitation, such as those associated with mining and plantations, settler farming and, eventually, labour-intensive manufacturing industries. Such a diversity of economic structures supports complex patterns of stratification consisting not merely of the colonial owners of economic enterprises and indigenous workers, who are held in varying degrees of subordination, but also many other groups. Divisions within the subordinate groups can generate intermediate categories, such as the Cape Coloureds in South Africa, or a whole range of colour castes that evolved in Mexico and Central America. Each possessed a certain level of rights and disabilities along the continuum stretching from the privileged colonial elite to the oppressed indigenous masses. Then there are the 'merchant minority' groups, such as the Indians, Chinese, Jews and Lebanese (Nicholls, 1981:415–31), discussed in more detail in chapter four. Finally, there are important divisions within the dominant colonial group between planters, settlers, administrators and missionaries, all with their own viewpoints and vested interests, which influence the power structure of colonial society.

Having outlined the enormous complexity of the colonial social structure, Rex proceeds to analyse the impact of dynamic changes upon it, giving particular attention to the forces of economic liberalization, moves towards political independence, the process of incorporation into the world system and internal class struggles and revolutions. It is against this background that the nature of race and ethnic relations in metropolitan societies can be interpreted, but not totally explained. For, as Rex is at pains to point out, this does *not* mean that 'there is no need to consider the mechanisms of assimilation and repulsion, of possible class alliance and class conflict, which actually occur in the metropolis' (ibid, 1981:5). In other words, Rex's paradigm emphasizes the colonial roots of so many patterns of race relations in both the Western capitalist and ex-colonial societies, but does not deny that each situation has certain unique dynamic properties of its own.

Thus the problems of race and ethnic relations arising in Britain and the industrial societies of North West Europe, based on immigration from former colonies or from the economically peripheral countries of the Mediterranean, differ in certain interesting respects from the position of blacks in the major cities of the USA. In the European case, immigrants have moved into welfare-state economies, capitalism modified by the power of organized labour, and this fact adds an important class dimension to the situation.[9] In the USA, blacks migrating from the South had to contend with a European immigrant labour force organized on ethnic lines, thereby creating a different milieu within which the struggle for full citizenship rights takes place. The interplay between class and ethnic identification emerges as an important aspect of these questions and 'class and ethnic community organization thus become alternative bases for immigrant organization' (1981:21).

Throughout his writings, Rex is insistent that he is conducting a class analysis of race relations, albeit one that incorporates a sophisticated appreciation of the many complexities involved. He is equally careful to allow a role for cultural distinctiveness and to concede that ideas, particularly racist ideas, may at certain stages take on a life of their own. This is essentially a Weberian analysis, a view of society that is an extension and modification of Marx's position rather than a 'refutation' of it (Weber, 1930:183; Giddens, 1970:303–5). That ideas play a special role in race relations has been recognized for a long time and can be seen in Rex's earlier definition of a 'race relations situation', which includes racist justifications and theories as an essential element (Rex, 1970:30; 136–61). The influence of Calvinist beliefs in shaping Afrikaner racial attitudes and behaviour in South Africa (Moodie, 1975; Adam & Giliomee, 1979:17–24); the possible role of Catholicism in the development of race relations in Latin America; and the impact of French culture, language and philosophy in France's colonies (Cohen, 1980) have all been the subject of considerable debate.

Rex's approach shares the same limitations that I have already noted with the models of van den Berghe and Lieberson, and critics might ask how applicable it is to race relations that have developed in non-colonial settings and in socialist societies. Others have claimed, erroneously in my opinion, that it underplays the reaction of minorities against oppression (Mason, 1982:433), which also reflects a broader objection to perspectives that place power relations at the centre of the analysis of society. In this chapter, I have emphasized power as a key concept in interpreting the evolution of race and ethnic relations, but this is not, of course, the only possible approach. There are many different ways of looking at society and more individualistic perspectives, such as those of the symbolic interactionists, as well as those using microeconomic analogies (notably Michael Banton's recent formulation of a 'rational choice' theory of race relations[10]), may also provide interesting insights. However, in my view, the most important single influence on the development of race and ethnic relations is the balance of power between different groups, and, while this may not totally determine the outcome, any convincing model must take the economic, social and political power realities as a starting point. Of these three dimensions one, the economic, has received a disproportionate amount of attention from scholars for a variety of reasons. I will consider whether this stance can be justified in the next chapter which will assess the Marxist contribution to the analysis of race and ethnic relations.

3 Race relations and class

Some social scientists would claim that the most distinctive contribution of Marxism to the study of race relations is to deny the existence of race relations at all. This is, in some measure, a variation on the argument proposed in my opening chapter which points to the spurious basis of biological theories of race relations. However, Marxist theories are generally far more specific than this, viewing racial and ethnic groups as an integral part of the class relations of society, and race, ethnic and national consciousness as examples of the 'false consciousness' of certain sections of the working class which have been deliberately misled by the propaganda of the bourgeois manipulators of ideas in capitalist society. The situation is, in reality, much more complicated than this because there are so many variations on a basic Marxist theme. In fact, 'Marxism' has played such an important role in the development of twentieth-century thought, and in the shaping of contemporary society, that it becomes almost meaningless to talk of it as a coherent and uniform body of thought. Marx's famous retort that he did not wish to be considered a Marxist reveals the extent to which his ideas had already become the subject of several interpretations during his lifetime.

The range and diversity of subsequent Marxist theory is almost as great as the variety of states and political movements that claim to be inspired by the ideals of the author of *Das Kapital* and *The Communist Manifesto* (Kolakowski, 1978: 3 vols.; McLellan, 1975). When one looks at the writings of prominent neo-Marxists in recent years this complex problem of relating class and race relations is apparent. Frantz Fanon, the theorist of the Algerian War of Independence, can be seen wrestling with the connection between national liberation strategies and socialist revolutions, both in Africa and in the rest of the Third World.[1] While Herbert Marcuse, a leading member of the Marxist-influenced Frankfurt School, argued that racial minorities, rather than the working classes of classical Marxism, would be in the vanguard of the revolutionary struggle to overthrow American capitalism.[2]

Part of the problem lies with Marx's own interpretation of these questions which, not surprisingly in a prolific author writing over a period of forty years, contained a number of ambiguities. Marx's principal preoccupation was with the nature of capitalist society and the manner in which it would be transformed, through the struggle between the owners of the means of production and the workers, into a socialist society. This was part of a broad evolutionary scheme, typical of much nineteenth-century social thought, which postulated a series of historical stages through which all societies must pass on the road to communism. The ancient world would lead into feudalism, which would then be overcome by capitalism which, in its turn, would succumb to the socialist revolution. An obvious objection to this approach is the manner in which it was heavily based on European historical experience, with vast tracts of the world, such as India and China, being dismissed on the grounds that they belonged to a separate and totally undynamic category which Marx called the 'Asiatic mode of production'. As Shlomo Avineri comments, 'stated bluntly it implies that Marx is aware of the fact that his philosophy of history does not account for the majority of mankind since it is relevant only to the European experience' (1968:11).

But even within European societies Marx's writings display considerable difficulties in reconciling the activities of racial, ethnic and national groups with his class-based model of social change. Marx's ambivalence in his analysis of the relationship between Irish nationalism and the English socialist movement is well known: he originally believed that an English proletarian revolution would produce a liberated Ireland, and later felt that Irish nationalism would act as the important catalyst that would ignite a class revolution in England. Marx and Engels's impatience with such ethnic and national complications to the class war is probably best captured in the latter's notorious outburst against the Irish worker in Manchester – 'his crudity places him little above the savage' (Foot, 1965:82). Subsequent distinctions drawn between the 'historic nations' of Western Europe and the 'ruins of peoples' to be found in Eastern Europe, as well as on the periphery of Western European states, give little assistance when trying to assess the strength of attachment to various nationalist forces. Thus, as Hélène Carrère d'Encausse rightly concludes, 'Marx and Engles left their followers little guidance in matters of nation and nationalism' (Calm & Fišera, 1980:114), and much the same is also true concerning race and ethnicity.

This problem has only become more apparent in the present century with Lenin's attempt to analyse imperialism as the 'highest stage' of capitalism, often resulting in a deplorable but very evident split in the labour movement, and Stalin's efforts to define, and later brutally resolve, the 'national question' in Soviet society.[3] It would seem, then, that Marxist analysis can easily founder on the rocks of racism and nationalism, but this does not mean that Marxist scholars have either ignored these issues, or, on occasions, have not made useful contributions to the debates that have been engendered by them. A distinction made between 'open Marxism' and the simplified dogmatic materialism, often referred to as 'vulgar Marxism', is helpful in differentiating between those Marxists who are prepared to recognize the complexity of racial and ethnic dynamics and those who simply dismiss the issues as irrelevant epiphenomena, a smokescreen disguising the 'objective' class relations which are the true cause of all social conflict. As Robert Blauner argues with respect to the United States:

. . . colonial forms of racial domination were entrenched in the matrix of a developing capitalism. A racial structure and a class structure were both produced. Races and classes coexist and interpenetrate. Racial division has influenced class formation and class factors have affected racial dynamics in a manner that a deterministic Marxism could not seriously investigate. (1973:35)

My own preference when considering these questions is to adopt a more general power analysis of race and ethnic relations as outlined in chapter two. While this approach recognizes the importance of economic factors, it regards the material base of society as one among several forces determining the extent and nature of racial and ethnic conflict. Perhaps the best way to assess the value of Marxist and neo-Marxist contributions to the study of race relations is to look at certain key problems where the scope and limits of a materialist perspective are highlighted with unusual clarity. Of these issues, I have selected three questions for closer scrutiny: the Marxist analysis of apartheid in South Africa; attempts to explain working-class racialism in Western industrial societies; and the experience of racial and national minorities in socialist societies.

At first sight, the attempt to analyse South African society – the most explicitly racist state in the contemporary world – in terms of class conflict would appear to be patently absurd. As Frank Parkin comments: 'to seek to impose class categories upon such a palpably racial system would seem to be somewhat akin to adopting a Parsonian integrationist model in the analysis of . . . modern Lebanon' (1979:38). And yet this is precisely what the neo-Marxist school of South African sociologists and historians have attempted in recent years. To these neo-Marxist scholars the conventional or 'liberal' interpretation of South African history, in terms of power struggles between racially defined groups, ignores the central role of capitalism in the creation and perpetuation of apartheid policies.[4] The influence of colonial conquest, slavery and the 'frontier tradition'; the ethnocentric heritage of Afrikaner nationalism; the alliance between white workers and Hertzog that first allowed the National Party to share power in 1924, and even the slogan of the South African Communist Party during the Rand Revolt (1922) – 'workers of the world fight and unite for a white South Africa' – are all seen as misleading 'superstructural' manifestations of an underlying 'objective' class reality.

While the neo-Marxists have been correct to attack the naive view that racial discrimination, and the whole migrant labour system, will inevitably collapse in the face of capitalist industrialization – an argument expressed by non-Marxist sociologists such as Herbert Blumer in the 1960s – their position goes further than this. For it is one thing to maintain that capitalist industry can coexist with job discrimination and racial segregation, strengthened and indeed more rigorously enforced after the Nationalist election victory in 1948, it is quite another matter to prove that such policies are the creation and the logical method of profit maximization for the capitalist sector of the South African economy. While the brutality of the pass laws, political disenfranchisement, restrictions on trade union organization and segregated education reduce the bargaining position of black workers by forcing down the price of African labour, this will tend to benefit agriculture and mining interests more than secondary manufacturing industry. In this sector, these measures restrict the growth of the black urban population which increases the scarcity, and hence the price of labour. Similarly, racial restrictive practices, reserving the skilled jobs for whites, increase white bargaining power and this in no way creates a situation designed to maximize the capitalists' profits. The obvious conclusion is that white workers are not a 'fraction' of the working class, temporarily seduced from their historic mission by capitalist-inspired racial delusions, but a distinct segment of society deliberately using racial boundary mechanisms as the most immediate means of improving their life chances. It is probably true to say that the white working classes, particularly the unskilled workers, have more to gain and less to lose from the perpetuation of the present system than the so-called capitalist architects of the apartheid state.[5]

This interpretation fits in with the split (or dual) labour

market theories proposed by some sociologists and economists to account for large differentials in the price of labour involved in the same occupations in multiracial societies. In developing a theory to explain different levels of ethnic antagonism, Edna Bonacich (1972:547–59) argues that such hostility 'first germinates in a labor market split along ethnic lines' (549). Ethnic and racial differences do not necessarily produce a split labour market if the various groups involved have similar resources and share similar goals when they enter the economic system. However, when these conditions do not prevail, a divergence between existing higher paid labour and cheaper labour sought by employers, either from abroad or from indigenous conquered groups, can lead to one of three basic results. The cheap labour can be substituted for higher priced labour to the benefit of the capitalists and to the detriment of the formerly higher paid workers; the cheap labour can be excluded by immigration restrictions; or, thirdly, an industrial caste system can be established producing the split labour market. The outcome will depend on the relative power of the higher paid labour group as compared to that of the employers, with the latter preferring the first solution, while the workers opt for the second or third. If the cheaper labour cannot be excluded, then higher paid labour will strive to create and maintain a reserved section of better paid jobs so becoming, in Lenin's famous phrase, 'an aristocracy of labour'.[6]

As we have seen, South Africa is an excellent example of this third pattern, with organized white labour buttressing its privileged position by all available means, economic, social, political and, on occasions, by the use of violence. White workers have tended to support laws and work practices aimed at preventing blacks from undercutting white wage rates; have been successful in monopolizing certain skills by denying educational and training resources to blacks; and have generally excluded them from trade unions. As Bonacich points out, the solution to 'the devastating potential of weak cheap labor is, paradoxically, to weaken them further, until it is no longer in business' immediate interest to use them as replacements' (1972:556). The other side of this argument is that rather than trying to protect this privileged section of the working class, business tends to support liberal or laissez-faire ideologies that would enable all workers, black and white, to compete freely in an open market. Backing given by major South African capitalists to the official opposition, the Progressive Federal Party, would seem to confirm this interpretation. It is only under duress that employers yield to the creation of a labour aristocracy. Generalizing from this situation, Bonacich concludes that a characteristic feature of societies with 'high levels of ethnic antagonism is that they all tend to have a powerful white (or more generally higher paid) working class' (ibid, 558).

The lessons of the South African case have been summarized by Heribert Adam who recognizes the economic component to the racial conflict in Southern Africa but, none the less, sees no reason to deny 'the independent role of beliefs' or the 'psychological functions of ethnic as opposed to class' identity (1979:46–50). He concludes that 'only a genuine synthesis of the interplay between ideology and economy, not the focus on either at the expense of the other, would seem to hold the key for deeper insights into this complex conflict' (ibid, 49–50). There is a need to recognize divisions within the white ruling groups, even within those labelled as 'capitalists', which may be important and represent genuine differences in interests. In other words, there may be more than one relationship to the means of production for those who nominally 'own' them, and conflicts in interests between the agricultural, mining, manufacturing and financial sectors, as well as between private and public enterprises. To regard the state as synonymous with, or a mere puppet of capitalist interests, is a crude oversimplification. There are also divisions within the 'objectively' defined working classes, particularly with regard to the political and legal status of black and white workers, producing profound barriers which have successfully undermined any semblance of class unity for more than half a century (Simons & Simons, 1969; Kuper, 1971 a).

*

If the Marxist analysis of South African society is particularly unsatisfactory, it nevertheless highlights those specific areas where the theory diverges most from reality. In contrast, we would expect a Marxist perspective to have greater validity in the class-stratified societies of Western Europe, the birthplace of modern capitalism. The emigration of migrant workers into Western Europe in the postwar period significantly increased the racial and ethnic diversity of these societies, whether the migrant labour force was derived from ex-colonies or from the peripheral economies of the Mediterranean basin. To what extent can the experiences of these migrant workers, their families and their children be understood in Marxian terms?

One attempt at such an analysis has been provided by Stephen Castles and Godula Kosack in their book *Immigrant Workers and Class Structure in Western Europe* (1973), which interpreted this massive migration as part of the process of international capitalist development. Immigrant workers are merely another element of the class structure of the host societies, forming a 'bottom stratum' of the working class because of their concentration in the least desirable manual occupations (1973:2–8). Ethnic differences between the very diverse sources of this migration are regarded as insignificant compared to their common structural location among the working classes, ethnic consciousness is dismissed as 'false consciousness', and working-class racism as a deliberately contrived mechanism of the ever-present and all-powerful 'ruling classes' to subvert the cause of working-class solidarity (1973:450–6). The evident entrepreneurial goals of several of these groups are largely ignored since 'objectively' they are defined as a 'working-class fraction' which should not aspire to become assimilated as part of the self-employed bourgeoisie.

Of course, many immigrant workers do share characteristics and conditions of the indigenous working classes: they may be trade union members, vote for labour, socialist or communist parties, and view their interests in class terms. But this does not mean that class, rather than ethnicity, will always be the more salient feature of the immigrant workers' organizational structure. Nor does it prevent the indigenous or white working classes from defining immigrants in racist terms and from believing, no matter how strong the evidence to the contrary, that they are the cause, rather than the victims, of economic and social problems.

A direct attempt to address these questions is presented by Annie Phizacklea and Robert Miles in their book *Labour and Racism* (1980), a study of black (largely West Indian) and white workers in Willesden, a poor, inner city area of north west London. Phizacklea and Miles are critical of what they call 'the race relations approach' of much sociological analysis of blacks in British society, singling out the work of John Rex and his collaborators (Rex & Moore, 1967; Rex & Tomlinson, 1979) for specific attack. This is somewhat ironic as Rex clearly regards his own work as a 'class analysis' and constantly repeats the claim. Phizacklea and Miles are also critical of the attempts by neo-Marxists like Poulantzas to incorporate intraclass divisions within a Marxist analysis of contemporary capitalism (*Classes in Contemporary Capitalism*, 1975), understandably feeling that the finer distinctions between 'categories', 'fractions' and 'strata' are ill-defined and often positively confusing. Nevertheless, they still argue that migrant labour in Britain must be seen as a 'fraction of the working class' (1980:23), and unfortunately they, too, fail to present us with a clear and unambiguous definition of what a 'fraction' actually is. The implication and continual assertion is that class will always override fractional alignments, although this is qualified by their recognition of the extent of racial discrimination and racism, not least among white workers (ibid, 156–7). The authors accept that these experiences of prejudice and discrimination may persuade black workers 'that their position as a racialized fraction of the working classes should serve as the basis for independent political action' and that this would be 'paralleled by the development of a particular form of political consciousness which we [will] . . . call *racial consciousness*' (ibid, :33–4, authors' emphasis).

Far from demolishing the value of a 'race relations' perspective on British racial and ethnic minorities, Phizacklea and Miles have demonstrated what an important qualification it provides to any class analysis.[7] Furthermore, if their sample evidence had not been so heavily based on the work relationships of the first generation of West Indians, and focused more on other groups, such as Asians, other areas, such as housing and education, and other generations, such as the British-born youth, then their position would have been even more difficult to sustain. Indeed, in the conclusion to their study they virtually concede the case when they argue:

We are therefore referring not to a potential but to a *real* source of fragmentation within black migrant labour as a working-class fraction, and this too must be recognized in any detailed analysis of political consciousness and action. (ibid, 231, my emphasis)

Stripped of its jargon, a 'Marxist' perspective on race and ethnic minorities in Western European, capitalist societies is rather similar to most other sociological analyses based on a broadly flexible theory of social stratification. When faced with North American race relations, Marxist scholars have encountered rather more difficulties in developing a convincing interpretation. During the high point of capitalist 'contradictions', the Great Depression of the 1930s, American communists pronounced themselves in favour of the creation of separate black states, a nationalist rather than a socialist solution to the 'race problem'.[8] This was based more on tactical orders from Moscow, fearing a racialist split in the ranks of organized labour, than on the logical development of socialist doctrine. In the postwar period, the leading theoretical text giving a 'Marxist' diagnosis of American race relations, Oliver Cox's *Caste, Class and Race* (1948), was, in fact, a highly idiosyncratic interpretation of Marxism, employing concepts such as 'political class', defined in a strikingly non- Marxist manner (Miles, 1980:169–87). It is hardly surprising that this work gave little assistance to those wishing to resolve the causal priority of class and racial variables in the USA, and Cox's later studies add more confusion, rather than help, in clarifying these issues (Stone, 1978:129–30).

None the less, some American scholars writing within the Marxist tradition, such as the historian Eugene Genovese, have departed a long way from a crudely materialist explanation of race relations in the United States (Genovese, 1971:333–56) and have roundly condemned other 'Marxists' for falling into this error. While discussing the various interpretations of the nature of slavery in the Americas, Genovese attacks the views of the anthropologist Marvin Harris because, 'what Harris' materialism, in contradistinction to Marxist materialism, fails to realize is that once an ideology arises it alters profoundly the material reality and in fact becomes a partially autonomous feature of that reality' (ibid, 1971:340). In other words, racial attitudes, ideologies and racial structures assume a life of their own and cannot be explained as the simple outcome of economic causes.

In order to understand the situation of the most oppressed racial minorities – blacks, Chicanos and American Indians – radical sociologists in America have tended to shift away from standard Marxian categories towards theories of 'internal colonialism' and dependency (Blauner, 1972; Barrera, 1979).[9] As I have already mentioned, some, like Marcuse, have been so disappointed by the lack of revolutionary consciousness on the part of the white working classes, and their evident racism, that they have completely abandoned the idea of a class struggle led by the classical Marxian proletariat comprising all industrial workers. The exploitation of American society is still seen as a capitalist conspiracy, but one that has been implemented with an enormous number of white working- class collaborators (Marcuse, 1964; 1969). The record of the labour unions has been one among several factors supporting this pessimistic (from a revolutionary standpoint) outlook (Lieberson, 1980:339–41; 358–9), and the total failure of the American Communist Party to attract anything more than a token number of black supporters gives little ground for accepting Marcuse's alternative scenario.

A more plausible account is suggested by Genovese (1968: 59–60) who argues that, no matter how much black suppression was linked to the capitalist structure of nineteenth-century America, after the second decade of the twentieth century capitalist organizations no longer required racial discrimination as a tool to maximize their exploitation of the American economy. However, like the spells of the sorcerer's apprentice, once set in motion racist ideologies, and the vested interest in the maintenance of a racial structure, took on a reality of their own so that the liberalization of American society along non-racial, universalistic lines has been a long and difficult battle, and one that has not primarily been opposed by organized business.

The struggle has been fought at least as much on a racial as on a class basis, with white workers, white trade union leaders, white grass-roots politicians and white policemen being equally, if not more, opposed to racial justice than the captains of industry. It would seem, therefore, that in order to understand the dynamics of race relations in the United States throughout the twentieth century, we need a theory that can explain, rather than explain away, these facts. While the necessary modifications to the Marxist model lead to the conclusion that the difference between an 'open Marxism' and a neo-Weberian approach to these questions boils down, apart from the political rhetoric, to a relatively minor matter of emphasis.

If Marxist sociology fails to predict the structure and outcome of race and ethnic relations under capitalism, how accurate is its analysis concerning the experience of minority groups in socialist states? More than one hundred years after the death of Marx, and some sixty-five years after the Russian revolution, can we observe the withering away of race and ethnicity under communist rule? The verdict is doubtful for there is considerable evidence to suggest that socialist states, both in the Eastern bloc and in the Third World, have not managed to eradicate national and ethnic loyalties, nor, indeed, are always free from some fairly blatant manifestations of racism. The situation is complicated because of the shifting tactical relationships between socialist and nationalist leaders. The position of the Jews in Russia since the middle of the nineteenth century illustrates these complex interrelationships, for the attitudes of the revolutionary left in Russia have changed quite significantly on several occasions (Goldhagen, 1977:273–86).

In the 1880s, the radical intelligentsia viewed the pogroms in a quite cynical light as the first step in the overthrow of the Tsarist regime. The Jews may not have deserved their fate at the hands of the peasants, but their blood would act as a 'lubricant on the wheels of revolution' (ibid, 275). To some extent, Marx's writings might appear to encourage this attitude. Although the real target of his attack was the capitalist system and not the Jewish capitalist *per se*, by identifying Jews in his famous essay *On the Jewish Question* with money and commerce, the epitome of capitalism, the message could easily be read in another way by those motivated more by anti-Semitism than by visions of social justice.

From the turn of the century until the 1920s, anti-Semitism was interpreted in a very different manner by Russian Marxists, being condemned by Plekhanov and Lenin as a Tsarist machination to divide the working classes and later as a counter-revolutionary ploy to restore the *ancien régime*. However, with the revival of Great Russian nationalism under Stalin, Marxist internationalism began to recede in the face of Russian chauvinism, and restrictions were placed on Jews limiting their access to the higher echelons of Soviet society, whether in educational, party, diplomatic or administrative positions. From 1948 until Stalin's death in 1953, these restrictions turned into wholesale persecution with the extinction of Jewish cultural institutions and the purging of leaders of the Jewish community. While the worst excesses ceased after Stalin's death, the restoration of cultural freedom did not take place for, as Goldhagen comments, 'the Jews are indeed a "chosen people" in Russia – chosen for cultural extinction' (1977:284).

The Soviet regime has tended to pursue a rather more pluralistic policy, at least in a cultural, if not in a political, sense, towards the other non-Russian nationality groups within the USSR. These groups make up one half of the total population of the country and, what is probably even more significant, are increasing at a faster demographic rate. However, this does not imply an absence of considerable tensions over policies that have been interpreted by many observers as russification, if not outright Russian imperialism (Pipes, 1975:453–65; Azrael, 1978). It is true that Lenin accepted the right to 'self-determination' of all national groups comprising the Soviet state, and that this included, at least in theory, the right to political secession and independence. However, like Marx, he believed that minorities under socialism would, of their own free will, prefer the economic benefits of integration in a larger, centralized workers' state. Ultimately there would be a fusion of nations, but this would only take place once the socialist revolution had run its course and had reached the final stage of the withering away of the state (Dreyer, 1976:48). During the transition to the true communist society, all nationalities should be formally equal, and minorities must be treated with sensitivity and tact to avoid any suspicion of Russian chauvinism. At first, Stalin was, if anything, even more emphatic than Lenin on the need to use minority languages and to preserve local national cultures. But this, too, was seen as a means to an end in which a common proletarian culture might appear in a number of national forms, but would still be socialist in content. The fact that this synthesis left any real conflicts between nationalism and socialism unresolved can be seen in the way in which Soviet minority policy developed in practice.

The 1924 Soviet Constitution recognized certain rights of national autonomy, including the right to secede and to be educated in the local language of a given region. Considerable efforts were made to mobilize the local populations and to modernize their economies through industrial development and collectivization. It was these measures that led to conflict and resistance so that by the 1930s Stalin's nationalities policy had changed to one of savage persecution. Local national elites were purged and largely replaced by Russians, and the powers of the union republics, the basic units of the Soviet federal system, were sharply curtailed. During the Second World War, seven entire nationality groups were deported to Siberia and Central Asia, on the grounds that some of their members were collaborating with the Nazi invaders, and millions died in labour camps (Kuper, 1981:96–9; 140–50). Only after Stalin's death, and with the rise of Khrushchev, was there a return to a less draconian nationalities policy, although this was combined with the large-scale colonization of the Central Asian republics by Russians. At first motivated by economic factors, the development of 'virgin lands', this was later continued as a result of strategic considerations, the border conflict with the Chinese. The present system incorporates tight control over centralized planning, with most crucial decisions being made in Moscow, while Russian immigrant party officials keep a close watch over local activities. Any outbursts of nationalist sentiment unacceptable to the Soviet regime are rigorously suppressed, although there is considerable evidence to suggest that there was a significant rise in national rights protests during the Brezhnev era (Kowalewski, 1981:175–88). Perhaps the most disruptive potential threat is in the ethnic composition of the Soviet army, with its overwhelming predominance of Russian officers commanding an expanding proportion of non-Russian rank and file, although there is little evidence as yet of any immediate danger to the unity of the Soviet state (Enloe, 1980:67–8).

The Soviet experience underlines the problems of trying to adapt national characteristics and cultures to a particular class-based model of society. An exercise in local autonomy that disturbs the designs of the Russian-dominated Central Committee of the Party can be quickly labelled as 'counter-revolutionary' activities, rather than the legitimate exercise of 'self-determination' under socialist federalism. More than half a century of Soviet rule has demonstrated quite clearly 'the difficulties inherent in a policy that aims at erasing ethnic differences by allowing them free rein' (Dreyer, 1976:60). It has also presented an ambiguous legacy for other Marxist-

Leninist states, raising as many questions as it answers. For, 'there are no clear guidelines on which minority group characteristics or forms must be erased in order to achieve a truly socialist content. Nor has any precise definition been worked out of which minority rights to support and to what extent' (ibid, 59).

These problems are not only the result of discrepancies between socialist theory and Soviet practice, but also a consequence of the ways in which Soviet policies have changed over the years. As a result, the leaders of the Chinese revolution had virtually to work out their own strategy towards the non-Han minorities of the Peoples' Republic. Mao Tse-tung's general statements describing the nationalities problem as basically a question of class provided no specific guidance as to which of the many different paths to follow that can be traced from the orthodox Marxian map. The earliest decision of the Chinese Communist Party was to adhere to the Leninist line of autonomy, together with the theoretical right to secession, but this was to change particularly in the light of fears generated by the problems of national security along the borders (Pye, 1975:494–503). While the policy of the Nationalist government before the Communist revolution was one of unification through assimilation, the Communists initially supported a much more pluralistic approach towards national minorities. After the Red Army's Long March, which took place through the territories of several of the minority populations, the Communist leadership began to realize the strength of distrust for Han power. As Lucian Pye comments: 'experience as contrasted to ideology was such that by the time the Communists came to power their earlier ideal of a federated state had given way to an appreciation of the value of a unitary state' (1975:495).

In the years after 1949, the Communist government's minority policy began increasingly to resemble the Nationalist model, varying somewhat according to changes in the influence of radical or conservative factions in the Party itself, to the degree of opposition of the minorities, and to perceived threats along its borders. Tibetan resistance was met by military force while in other border areas, such as the Inner Mongolian and Uighur Autonomous Regions, control from Peking was strengthened by an expansion of the centralized administrative structure and the encouragement of massive migrations of Han settlers. On the surface, the Communists paid lip service to minority autonomy, but their actions displayed a preference for bureaucratic centralization and sinification, which was further reinforced after the Sino-Soviet rift in 1960, and the subsequent border clashes with the Russians. Although only six per cent of the total Chinese population is of non-Han ethnicity, these peoples occupy nearly ninety per cent of the territories bordering on China's neighbours.

June Dreyer sums up the dilemmas facing Chinese national strategy in the following terms:

The twists and turns of party policy over the past quarter century may be seen as an effort to find a balance between destroying minority group characteristics slowly enough to avoid arousing minorities' antagonism, yet quickly enough to prevent the accretion of vested interests that might become strong enough to halt the destruction in mid-course. (1976:272)

China's experience with its minority peoples, like those of its Soviet neighbour, must destroy any naive belief that minority national identity would simply collapse when faced by a homogeneous proletarian culture. Whatever the eventual outcome in the world's two major communist states, it is clear that the path to socialist integration is going to be a long and tortuous one.

However, it is not only the communist superpowers that have faced significant difficulties in trying to resolve the dialectic between nationalism and socialism. Smaller socialist states have encountered similar problems with their ethnic and national minorities. Yugoslavia, during and after the Tito era, has experienced considerable ethnic tensions not only between the Serbs and the Croats, the two largest ethnic communities, but also with several of the smaller national groups like the Albanians (Karlovic, 1982:276–99). After a careful consideration of the way in which the Serbian elite of the Yugoslav Communist Party has managed to dominate and to systematically exploit the other nationalities and regions of the state, Karlovic claims that this may be described as another case of 'internal colonialism', quite as oppressive as the ethno-regional exploitation to be found in capitalist societies. In fact, he argues that the structure of a Marxist regime provides even less opportunity for compromise than a democracy, 'particularly in the area of power-sharing with nationalists from the periphery who are not party members and who, as a consequence, must be excluded from any solution' (1982:292). In general, his evidence supports my argument that nationalism cannot simply be explained in material terms:

To view ethnic nationalism as merely a superstructure of an economic base, or as a smokescreen for economic demands, is misleading; by the same token, to attempt to disengage the two is unhelpful. As much as body and soul, they co-exist and feed upon each other. Economic exploitation serves to sensitize individuals in the periphery to the existence of ethnic differences and to feel discontent along ethnic lines. This is particularly significant in an authoritarian state . . . (ibid, 293)

A final example illustrating that it is not only Marxist-Leninist states, but also Marxist-inspired liberation movements, that encounter these ethnic complications can be taken from the small West African state of Guinea-Bissau. In this case, the principal liberation movement, the PAIGC, which had been inspired by Marxist ideologies, was founded and led by Amilcar Cabral from the early 1950s until his assassination in 1973, one year before his organization finally won the liberation struggle against the Portuguese colonial power. Cabral's views shared the orthodox Marxist approach towards ethnic and racial divisions during a class-based revolution, tolerating cultural diversity provided that it was contained within strict political limits. Cabral believed that 'the liberation struggle itself would provide the crucible to melt away most ethnic differences' (Lyon, 1980:157).

Guinea-Bissau was a typical African state constructed by the colonial powers with absolutely no regard to ethnic or cultural unity. It therefore contained a large number of different ethnic groups of which four were of predominant importance: the Balanta and related peoples (comprising 49 per cent of the total population), the Fula (22 per cent), the Manjaco (14 per cent), and the Mandinga (13 per cent). In contrast, the leadership of the PAIGC, including Cabral, consisted of 'assimilados' drawn from the small commercial and civil service elite, a group whose mixed ancestry predisposed them towards a non- tribal, universalistic outlook which also harmonized with their Marxian political philosophy. As Judson Lyon comments, Cabral's understanding of ethnic or national ties as they functioned in Africa was an 'intellectual and not an emotional one' (ibid, 158).

The initial attempt to organize the tiny working class of the colony, following a Marxist rather than a Maoist strategy, was met with bloody suppression, and this forced the PAIGC to try to mobilize the peasantry. The party started this work among the Balanta, implicitly recognizing the importance of ethnicity in the loyalties of the Guinean people, and was careful to use Balanta, or Balanta-trained cadres in mobilizing the rural population in these regions. The policy met with considerable success, but the attempts to enlist the support of the other ethnic groups proved to be much more complicated. It is true that this was partly because of the Portuguese tactics of promoting tribal divisions in order to perpetuate their rule, but it was also a result of genuine historical animosities and rivalries between the different groups.

Large sections of the Fula and Manjaco remained outside the movement, or in opposition to it, throughout the struggle. The Mandinga only began to support the PAIGC on a significant scale in the early 1970s, and this was not simply a desire to rid themselves of Portuguese rule, nor a conversion to the Marxist vision of the party. The underlying motivation seems to have been fear of their traditional enemies, the Fula, whom the Portuguese had belatedly decided to train and arm as an African commando force. After independence there has been evidence of continuing ethnic strife and claims of inequitable land redistribution, and certainly ethnic divisions have not disintegrated, as Cabral prophesied they would, with the end of colonialism. It would seem that the success of Cabral's movement may well have been due to 'its ability to mobilize peoples on an ethnic basis, rather than a socio-economic one, all its protests notwithstanding' (Lyon, 1980:166).

Marxist theorists have been keen to emphasize the unity of theory and practice. In this chapter, I have tried to show how the deficiencies in the Marxist theory of race and nationalism are clearly reflected in the practical difficulties faced by rulers of Marxist-Leninist states and by the leaders of Marxist-inspired movements in both capitalist and Third World societies.[10] Nevertheless, it would be wrong to suggest that there is no value at all in a Marxist perspective, provided that it is used in a flexible, 'open' manner and applied to those situations where economic variables are particularly important. It is hardly surprising that many students of social change in Central and South America have found class-based theories to be of special value. This is because many of the societies in these regions have become increasingly polarized on class lines, while racial and ethnic divisions, as a result of a complex accumulation of historical causes, have begun to assume a rather low profile (van den Berghe, 1978a:xxvi).

However, there are many situations where granting causal priority to material factors is not simply a distortion of the truth, but totally misleading. It is my position that Marxism may be subsumed under a more general power analysis of relations between groups in society, and that the economic dimension is *one* important, though not necessarily predominant, element in the total picture. The fact that Marxist theories, like most theories of revolution, were 'derived from an analysis of conflict between social classes in racially homogeneous societies' (Kuper, 1971a:87) should lead us to expect that they may result in a certain measure of ethnocentric bias if applied in other contexts. When attempting to understand phenomena as persistent and complex as ethnicity and nationalism, it is sensible to heed Hugh Seton-Watson's perceptive warning:

Devotion to a national identity is not a temporary by-product of class conflict or economic frustration, though either of these can aggravate it, but something deep-rooted, which has to be respected if the human race is to escape disasters. (1982:13)

In the next chapter, I will consider whether other major theories of social change, including some formulated specifically with racial and ethnic diversity as a basic premise, can provide a more convincing explanation of the dynamics of racial and ethnic change in both the developing and developed world.

4 Race relations and social change

If Marxist theories of race relations have made the mistake of overemphasizing the economic dimension of race and ethnic problems, these are not the only theories to have fallen into this trap. I will now assess the extent to which non-Marxist theories of 'modernization'[1] have made a similar error while trying to account for changing patterns of race and ethnic relations. Then I will consider whether a totally different concept, that of the 'plural society', might not provide a better understanding of the relationships between ethnic and racial groups in Third World societies. Finally, I will re-examine the belief that the developed countries are actually as homogeneous as is sometimes assumed in much of the literature on modernization, by looking more closely at what has been called the 'ethnic revival' in the Western world.

Other prominent schools of thought within social and political science seem to share the Marxist view that racial and ethnic identification is ultimately subservient to economic and technological change. There is a certain irony in this since many of these scholars are clearly hostile to Marxism, both as a political philosophy and as an intellectual system. Theories of 'modernization' proposed by political scientists during the 1950s and 1960s (Deutsch, 1953; Apter, 1965), and equally by sociologists at about the same time (Bell, 1960; Parsons, 1966), seemed to share with Marxism the assumption about the diminishing significance of race and ethnicity in the modern world. These predictions were applied universally, to the post-colonial Third World as well as to the major capitalist and socialist societies, and in all three cases they have proved to be, if not completely false, at least premature (Stone, 1982:85–99).

Two influential critiques of these modernization and 'nation-building' theories can be found in the writings of Herbert Blumer (1965) and Walker Connor (1972). Blumer's criticisms were levelled at those arguments that select one dimension of modernization, the impact of industrialization, and suggest that, as societies become increasingly industrialized, forces are unleashed that will inevitably break down barriers between racial and ethnic groups. In reality, the argument appeared in many different forms and was in no way confined to the relations between racial groups. It could be seen, for example, in two parallel theories: the *embourgeoisement* thesis, which claimed that industrialism eroded class consciousness and destroyed class barriers; and the *convergence* thesis, which maintained that capitalist and communist societies were becoming increasingly alike in the 'post-industrial' world (Goldthorpe, 1964; Goldthorpe et al., 1969).

No one would deny the importance of industrialization as a central force influencing modern society, but whether it is capable of shaping social stratification or moulding political institutions and ideologies *according to a single and specific pattern* is another matter. The same is true concerning its impact on race and ethnic relations. According to Blumer, sociologists who believe that there are certain 'logical imperatives' associated with industrialism usually stress a series of interrelated factors.[2] Industrialism requires a commitment to a rational and secular outlook which is needed for productive efficiency and profitability. This leads to the substitution of contractual relationships for status relationships so that employees at all levels within the industrial enterprise are judged according to their skills and expertise, rather than because of their membership of a specific class or because of their racial or ethnic background. Furthermore, industrialism promotes impersonal markets of which the labour market is crucial so that 'employees are not tied to jobs nor are jobs vested in employees'. Similarly, industrialism needs and promotes social mobility so undermining 'status by ascription' and replacing it with 'status by achievement'. This mobility affects both employees and entrepreneurs: the latter who operate efficient enterprises accumulate and attract capital for further investment and expand, while the inefficient are forced into bankruptcy. Taken together these factors generate a dynamic social system which is constantly adjusting to changes in technology and shifts in consumer demand.

From this particular standpoint, industrialism transforms society by undermining the traditional social order. And by throwing people into new situations, it creates new patterns of social relationships. As a result, so the argument runs, it establishes a new type of society based on the 'intrinsic' features of industrialization. What, then, according to this conventional view, is the precise impact of the process of industrialization on race relations? One argument maintains that industrialization destroys the established structure of race relations by attacking it directly in the ways outlined above, but also by disturbing the existing order of society, thereby challenging the racial status quo. However, there is little empirical evidence to support the claim that this is necessarily the outcome and many dominant groups manage to manipulate and steer industrialism in ways which are perfectly compatible with, or indeed may actually strengthen, the traditional power structure.

Managers of industrial plants wishing to hire employees on a colour-blind basis can be prevented from doing so by objections, or the fear of such objections, from other workers. This may be a perfectly rational decision from the employer's standpoint and frequently occurs in areas where industrialism has been introduced into a society with a strongly established racial hierarchy. The same may be true with regard to the promotion of well-qualified members of subordinate groups and the employment of minorities in positions where they are exposed to public prejudice, such as sales personnel, receptionists and outside representatives of the organizations. Blumer comments:

These are typical kinds of rational decisions – decisions which are guided just as much by the aim of efficient operation and economic return as if they took into account only the productive capacity of the individual racial member. They show clearly that *rational* operation of industrial enterprises which are introduced into a racially ordered society may call for a deferential respect for the canons and sensitivities of that racial order. (1965 in 1977:160)

There are many examples of this type of interracial behaviour under colonial regimes, in South Africa and, until recently, in the Southern states of America (Stone, 1973:39–44). The rational response of industrial enterprises in these circumstances is as often to act in a manner that supports, rather than undermines, the existing racial order. A closer regard for the actual evidence, rather than a reliance on *a priori* theoretical arguments, suggests that similar conclusions are true with respect to all of the 'logical' imperatives of industrialism. The movement from status relationships to contractual relationships in the early phases of industrialization does not necessarily result in a corresponding change in the racial hierarchy. An individual's racial status can override his contractual status so, for example, confining subordinate workers to the more menial and lower paid jobs in the industrial economy. Similarly, it can restrict minority entrepreneurs to a limited and relatively unprofitable sphere of industrial and commercial activities. In Blumer's words: 'the whole texture of the new contract relations may reproduce and continue the social position of the races' (1965 in 1977:160). Identical conclusions can be reached with regard to the increased physical mobility which accompanies industrialization. People may move but they are likely to remain in segregated neighbourhoods which merely recreate the pre-existing racial order in a different spatial setting. As for social mobility, while it may increase as a result of the expanding opportunities of an industrial society, this does not mean that the structural alignment of racial groups necessarily changes. The industrial history of South Africa has shown that job reservation can persist for decades under such conditions, and that substantial economic growth can take place without altering the relative material advantages of one group as compared to another.

The implication of these observations is that industrialization operates in a far more complicated way than is conventionally assumed. Pronouncements about its effect on patterns of race relations have placed too much weight on a process of deductive reasoning from certain theoretical premises and have not been based on a careful assessment of the evidence concerning actual types of group behaviour. A more realistic perspective must recognize that industrialization and race relations act on each other, that their interaction is profoundly affected by the context in which it occurs, and that this setting is also influenced by broad social and political factors (Blumer, 1965 in 1977:164). Both industrialization and racial relationships are highly complicated processes and a balanced assessment must therefore view industrial development as a stimulant to change, without being dogmatic about the precise direction in which this change will lead.

Similar conclusions have been reached by Walker Connor in relation to a parallel argument accepted by many political scientists during the 1950s and 1960s. Connor shows how many American political scientists, particularly those following the admittedly ambiguous writings of Karl Deutsch, have tended to 'slight, if not totally ignore, problems associated with ethnic diversity' (Connor, 1972 in 1977:238). This bias could only be justified on the grounds that modern states[3] are either ethnically and racially homogeneous, or that such diversity as they do possess would in no way threaten their political and social unity. A closer scrutiny of these assumptions reveals that both are incorrect. For not only are ethnically homogeneous states the exception rather than the rule – in almost thirty per cent of contemporary states the largest ethnic group does not even constitute one half of the total population – but also in many of the multi-ethnic states conflicts between the various communities pose the greatest single challenge to their continued existence. There is plenty of evidence to support the proposition that ethnic consciousness has not decreased as a result of the major processes that make up the components of modernization, simply by noting the number of ethnic nationalist movements that are thriving in advanced industrial societies. Can we therefore argue the opposite case and suggest that ethnic mobilization has actually increased as a result of modernization?

Connor is cautious on this point and makes the following assessment:

> . . . there is a danger of countering the assumption that the processes of modernization lead to cultural assimilation with an opposing iron law of political disintegration which contends that modernization results, of necessity, in increasing demands for ethnic separation. We still do not have sufficient data to justify such an unequivocal contention. Nonetheless, the substantial body of data which is available supports the proposition that material increases in what Deutsch terms social communication and mobilization *tend* to increase cultural awareness and to exacerbate inter-ethnic conflict. (1972 in 1977:244)

This is because advances in transport and communications, core elements in modernization, increase the awareness of various minority groups of their distinct cultural or ethnic identity and the threat posed to its survival by the closer integration of the state. Paradoxically, the very success of the state in exercising its influence over all regions and groups within its borders, its control over the mass media and its direction of language policies and education, is not simply a force for integration and assimilation of minorities into the dominant culture and political system. The state's growing power to make decisions and, above all, to implement them, has an important impact on local life and community affairs. It can easily be interpreted as a direct threat to the survival of the minority as a separate entity. Some of the resources available to political leaders to strengthen centralized control can also be employed by nationalist and regionalist groups in efforts to secure greater autonomy or, in the extreme case, to break away and establish independent states of their own. Thus so-called 'nation-building', which in precise language should be called *state*-building, is, in reality, an attempt at 'nation-destroying' (Connor, 1978:377–400). For the integration of the state requires some transference of loyalty from the ethnic group (or nation) to the wider state organization. In many respects, therefore, such a policy is a two-edged sword that can have unanticipated consequences diametrically opposed to the original designs of the state-builders.

There are many complex reasons why theorists of 'nation-building' have tended to downplay the role of ethnicity in their analyses of contemporary social change. Connor suggests a number of plausible explanations. Many writers have underestimated the emotional power of nationalism – often as a result of misunderstanding its essential nature. Nationalism, so Connor would argue, is at root a matter of psychological identity with a particular group but is frequently associated with a number of tangible traits such as religion, language or physical location. No one would deny the importance of Judaism in the maintenance of Jewish nationalism, or Catholicism's role in Irish, Polish or Quebec nationalism. However, while religion may be a symbol of nationalism, it is not its essential characteristic, and this explains the persistence of nationalist feeling even after a substantial period of secularization. The decline in the power and influence of the Catholic Church in Quebec has taken place at a time of intensified nationalist sentiment. Much the same is true in the case of language and nationalism. The fading influence of Gaelic since the foundation of Eire does not signify the demise of Irish nationalism.

Another reason for the false diagnosis of ethnicity and nationalism is the exaggerated stress on materialism that I have discussed at length in the last chapter. There have also been a number of mistaken assumptions and false analogies that have added to the confusion. The argument that greater intergroup contact necessarily means greater assimilation is a matter of wishful thinking rather than a careful assessment of the evidence on intergroup relations. As Connor wryly comments: 'while the idea of being friends presupposes knowledge of each other, so does the idea of being rivals' (1972 in 1977:254). This is a mistake that parallels the error often made by naive liberals who believe that interracial contacts *per se* break down racial stereotypes. In reality, it is only in the rather special case where there are equal status contacts under non-competitive conditions that this outcome is at all likely. Greater contacts in a racially stratified situation may well *reinforce*, rather than undermine, negative group images.

Further confusion has arisen from the tendency to use the ethnic experience of the United States (or, at least, one interpretation of it) as a suitable model for an assessment of the normal pattern of ethnic assimilation. Despite the 'white ethnic revival' of the 1970s, the assimilative powers of American society have been remarkably strong. This is because the pressure to assimilate has come from successive waves of voluntary migrants, rather than from the dominant white, Anglo-Saxon population. (The case of blacks, and of black nationalism, is, of course, the notable exception.) However, where the situation is reversed so that the pressure to assimilate is viewed by a minority as coming from the majority, this can produce fears of 'cultural imperialism' and result in determined resistance. This is, in fact, the more normal setting for ethnic conflict and one for which the American experience is quite misleading. It certainly can tell us little about the separatist attitudes of many French Canadians in Quebec, to cite just one example. In most cases, assimilation is a long drawn out process which is more likely to succeed when it is carried out slowly, over centuries, rather than in the sociological pressure cookers created by modern 'nationalist' leaders intent on rapid state-building. Nor is assimilation an inevitable, one-way process: there is a dialectic of fusion and fission that marks the ethnic history of most eras (Stone, 1976:27).

One final problem is simply a confusion in terminology: the state is a political unit, while the nation is the ethnic group with which an individual identifies. The two terms are not identical although both scholars and people in general tend to use them as if they were interchangeable. As I have already pointed out, there are often several nations in a state and the confusing term 'nation-state' is literally true in only a small minority of cases. Similarly, by reserving the term 'nationalism' for loyalty to the state, identification with the nation has had to be described by a variety of other terms such as ethnicity, regionalism, communalism or tribalism. This has resulted in a dangerous underestimation of the power and resilience of ethnic identity and has diverted attention away from the fundamental question of the conflict between ethnic and state loyalties (Rothchild & Olorunsola, 1982). As Connor asks: 'would scholars have been less sanguine concerning the chances of success of [state-building] if proper terminology had been employed? Certainly they would have been less likely to ignore, or dismiss lightly, the problems of ethnic identity, the true nationalism' (1972 in 1977:249–50).

From this discussion of the impact of modernization and industrialization on racial and ethnic groups, it is clear that divisions of race and ethnicity remain major features of most modern societies. The argument advanced by certain sociologists that they should be regarded as a residual or 'secondary' component of the social structure (Lockwood, 1970:58) is based on a model of society that, by definition, relegates race and ethnicity to a subordinate conceptual status. While the reasons for this bias may be found in the legacy of nineteenth-century social theory, the justification for its persistence cannot be discovered in the relations and conflicts of modern society. There has been, of course, a significant minority of social scientists who have long maintained that these divisions are fundamental social facts and that they have been closely associated with what may be called the tradition of the 'plural society'.

The term 'plural society' originated in the writings of J. S. Furnivall, whose studies were based on research in the colonial tropical territories of South East Asia, and in particular Indonesia and Burma (Furnivall, 1948). Furnivall's original formulation of the concept was part of a general theory of capitalist colonialism in which economic forces generated by Western political expansion interacted with traditional Eastern societies to form a unique type of social system. This 'plural society' comprised separate communities distinguished by sharp racial, ethnic and linguistic divisions, sharing no common will, and united only by the impersonal contacts in the market place and the overarching colonial political structure. Furnivall recognized that many societies possessed plural features, but this in itself did not make them plural societies. The plural society had a combination of unique qualities which resulted in a profound potential for instability. In *Colonial Policy and Practice*, his major book on the subject, he described the crucial features of what was clearly a very special type of social system:

> . . . the plural society is built on caste without the cement of a religious sanction. In each section the common social will is feeble, and in the society as a whole there is no common social will. There may be apathy even on such a vital point as defence against aggression. Few recognize that, in fact, all the members of all the sections have material interests in common, but most see that on many points their material interests are opposed. The typical plural society is a business partnership in which, to many partners, bankruptcy signifies release rather than disaster. (Furnivall, 1948:307)

Above all, the colonial political structure allowed market forces to run riot without any of the social inhibitions found in those Western societies which had been the birthplace of capitalism:

> In the first half of the nineteenth century economists eulogized economic man; in the last half they said he was a myth. Unfortunately they were mistaken. When cast out of Europe he found refuge in the tropics, and now we see him returning with seven devils worse than himself. These are the devils that devastated the tropics under the rule of *laissez-faire* and which it is the object of modern colonial policy to exorcise. (ibid, 311)

Furnivall's vivid portrait of a society divided into exclusive racial and ethnic segments has been extended, and subtly modified, by many subsequent social scientists. In particular, M. G. Smith developed the concept in relation to the multi-ethnic and multiracial societies of the Caribbean and Africa (Smith, 1965; Kuper & Smith, 1969). Smith distinguished between three major types of society, which he called 'homogeneous', 'heterogeneous' and 'plural', according to the extent to which they were differentiated in their major social institutions. Where this was minimal, the society could be regarded as homogeneous from a racial and ethnic standpoint. Where differentiation occurred at the secondary level, in a society's religious, economic and political institutions, then this produced a heterogeneous society. And where differences extended to the 'basic' level, in the family, patterns of socialization and other small-scale, intimate relationships, this resulted in a truly plural society.

Thus societies like the United States, which Smith would classify as heterogeneous and which clearly consist of a wide range of racial and ethnic groups, could be distinguished from the plural societies of Asia, Africa and the Caribbean. Smith also introduced a further criterion for separating plural societies from other multiracial societies, and this is the process by which groups are integrated into the society. Integration can assume three major forms: 'differential incorporation' which involves the domination of one group by another; 'consociation' which consists of two or more groups integrating on an equal basis; and 'universalism' where rights and privileges are granted on an individual basis unrelated to group membership (Kuper & Smith, 1969:434-5).

Smith's analysis helps to place the concept of the plural society within the wider context of racial and ethnic diversity. It is clear that Furnivall's preoccupation with the study of colonial race relations made him construct a model that was too restricted in both time and space. For pluralism was not confined to the tropics nor to the era of European colonialism, as the examples of plural societies in the long-independent states of Latin America and in South Africa testify. More generally, plural society theory has been criticized because, it is claimed, it tends to ignore, or underemphasize, other types of cleavage, such as class divisions, in its concentration on racial and ethnic subcommunities. It has also been argued that 'pluralism' is better regarded as a continuous variable, present to a greater or lesser degree in all societies, rather than seen as the property of a distinctive type of society (Cross, 1971:477-94). Furthermore, some critics dismiss it as little more than a classificatory scheme and one that fails to set out the dynamic properties of racially divided societies.

While there is some truth in all of these points, I do not believe that they invalidate the concept of a society where racial and ethnic divisions are of paramount significance, and where political and economic cleavages are continually translated into racial and ethnic terms. That this need not be confined to colonial and ex-colonial societies of the Third World is perfectly true, and John Thompson has convincingly demonstrated that a plural society analysis of Northern Ireland provides a better explanation of the dynamics of contemporary Ulster than either developmental or neo-Marxist models (Thompson, 1983:127–53). Indeed, the claim that theories of pluralism and the plural society, which stress cleavages between sections of society differentiated on the basis of race and ethnicity, should be set alongside Marxist revolutionary theories and neo-Durkheimian theories of evolutionary change as the major theoretical interpretations of political change in multiracial societies, seems well justified (Kuper, 1971b: 594–607). In many cases plural society theories appear to provide a better appreciation of the power realities and the structure of conflict in these societies than either the Marxist or Durkheimian models.

The main problem with which we are faced is to present a clearer outline of the dynamics of plural societies, and here a crucial issue is the extent to which major cleavages within these societies are superimposed on each other. This has been recognized for a long time as a critical factor in determining the violence and intensity of class conflict in industrial societies (Dahrendorf, 1959:210–18), and the same insight can be applied equally to the situation of racial and ethnic conflict. Where there is an absence of cross-cutting cleavages, so that racial and ethnic divisions within a society also correspond to differences in economic, social and political power (including the military and bureaucratic strength of contending groups), then we can explain two characteristic, and superficially paradoxical, features of plural societies. On the one hand, plural societies may be subject to long periods of relative stability where the suppression of the subordinate groups by the dominant elite is so comprehensive that resistance is futile and can be easily crushed. On the other hand, once violence does break out on a significant scale it tends to escalate rapidly, spreading to include economic, political and social grievances, and taking on an intensity and savagery of its own. The sources of the earlier cohesion become the battlelines of the subsequent conflict. Thus, what Furnivall developed as a theory to explain colonial tropical societies has, with suitable adaptation, great relevance for our understanding of the nature of many contemporary racial and ethnic conflicts, such as those found in the Lebanon, Northern Ireland and South Africa.[4]

One common feature of many plural societies is the presence of middlemen or merchant minorities. These minorities may be defined as ethnic or racial groups occupying an intermediate position in the stratification system of multiracial societies by virtue of their specialist economic activities. The Chinese in South East Asia, the Jews in Europe, Indians in East and Southern Africa, Armenians in Turkey, and the Japanese and Chinese in the United States, being typical examples of this social form. Such groups are of considerable interest because they do not fit into the standard pattern of ethnic and racial subordination, and yet they are found in so many societies throughout the world that they cannot be dismissed as isolated exceptions to the normal form of ethnic stratification. Furnivall noted the hostility felt towards such groups in South East Asia:

In Burma the Indian and Chinese middleman form combines against the cultivator and the European miller . . . In Java the nationalist movement first assumed a popular character in action against the Chinese, whom Europeans at the same time were describing as worse than ten epidemics. In Indo-China Annamese and Europeans regard the Indian moneylender as a pest . . . (1948:310)

He interpreted their characteristic activities as yet another manifestation of the amoral nature of colonialism, a view endorsed by other scholars analysing the era of colonial rule in South East Asia who have sometimes attributed the position of middleman minorities to the deliberate machinations of the imperial rulers (Abraham, 1983:18–32).

However, the form of middleman minority appears in so many different types of society that it cannot be claimed to be the exclusive consequence of colonial manipulation. In fact, the archetypal middleman minority was the Jew in European society, whose special characteristics were distilled by Georg Simmel in his famous essay on 'The Stranger' (Stone, 1977:13–17). For Simmel, the stranger was not defined as 'the wanderer who comes today and goes tomorrow', but rather as 'the person who comes today and stays tomorrow'. He was a *potential* wanderer, an individual who lived in a society but who was not fully a part of it. Such a marginal position has a number of economic and social consequences which means that the stranger is ideally suited to fulfil the role of the middleman minority. A central characteristic, described by several scholars as 'sojourning', is a quality emphasized by Edna Bonacich in her initial attempt to outline a general theory to explain middleman minorities (1973:583–94).

Several basic explanations are usually advanced to account for the origin and persistence of middleman minorities. It is argued that the hostility of the dominant group in a society prevents access to the most desirable economic roles which results in the minority group closing ranks and making exceptional efforts to achieve economic success. A second factor stressed is the special nature of the society in which middleman groups are typically found, particularly a marked status gap between the elite rulers and the masses. Such a gulf existed between the peasants and landed aristocracy in feudal Europe, and between the indigenous peoples and the settler rulers in colonial societies. Middleman minorities were able to fill this gap and act as ideal intermediaries between the elites and the masses. This is because they lacked the status inhibitions of the surrounding society which enabled them to trade and have dealings with all groups in a free and impartial manner. Secondly, they do not have the family and other kinship ties than can interfere with, or otherwise impede, their trading activities. And thirdly, they can act as a political buffer between the elite and the masses, occupying highly visible and often conflict-laden roles, such as small shopkeepers, money-lenders and tax collectors, which accounts for the displaced aggression that they often attract (Bonacich, 1973:584).

These two factors, however, cannot explain why the hostility of the host society results in the closing of ranks of these particular minorities rather than forcing them to the bottom of the economic system. Nor can it account for the persistence of this social form long after the status gaps have been eroded, as in post-colonial states or in modern industrial societies which have developed beyond their feudal social origins. Bonacich argues that the answer to these questions lies in the fundamental orientation of the groups concerned, that as sojourners they originally never intended to remain in the society on a permanent basis. Consequently, middleman minorities are industrious and are prepared to work long, anti-social hours precisely because their reference group is not the society in which they are living. They are thrifty, saving rather than consuming the wealth they accumulate, and selecting, wherever possible, occupations which allow for geographical mobility. In general, they avoid industrial enterprises which require long-term capital investment, preferring instead restaurants, laundries, shops selling jewellery or the independent professions. The only type of agricultural pursuit that is at all common is market gardening, where there is a rapid yield and turnover.

All these characteristics can be related to the longer term goal of returning or retiring to some ancestral or former homeland. In addition, middleman minorities are noted for the strength of their internal group solidarity which leads to complex patterns of mutual aid and trust. These are reinforced by the desire to maintain distinctive community organizations, such as language and religious schools. There is often a strong resistance to intermarriage, a preference for residential self-segregation, and a tendency to avoid political involvement except on issues that specifically affect community interests.

While sojourning is an important element in the development of this type of minority it is not the only cause of the middleman form. Many sojourning migrant labourers do not become small businessmen and there is a marked tendency for certain groups, particularly the Jews, Chinese and Indians, to become middleman minorities wherever they go. This would suggest that certain cultural traits may be an important additional factor, and that a status gap within a relatively hostile host society may be a necessary, but hardly a sufficient condition to produce this result. Some would even challenge the importance of the hostile environment, citing the cases of the Parsis in traditional Hindu caste society and the Japanese in Brazil, as examples of middleman minorities who did not have to face significant antagonism (Stryker, 1974:281–2).

It could be claimed that the political context, and particularly the role of emergent nationalism, better explains the heightened level of hostility and persecution suffered by these minorities. Bonacich has refined this argument by suggesting that it is the relative power of those groups most likely to be in competition with the middleman minorities that will determine the intensity of the conflict (Bonacich, 1974:282). Nevertheless, sojourning is an important factor as most middleman minorities were not involved in business activities in the societies from where they emigrated, often because these roles were already monopolized by other middleman minority groups. Thus the only route towards economic advancement for groups displaced from their traditional agricultural employment lay in the diaspora.

The problem of explaining the origin and persistence of middleman minority groups is complex, and in a more recent attempt to provide a comprehensive account of the phenomenon Turner and Bonacich (1980:144–58) have stressed three sets of basic variables. These are: *cultural* variables, related to the distinctive characteristics of the migrant minority; *contextual* variables, concerning the properties of the host society; and *situational* variables, focusing on the sojourning or stranger role itself. In order to develop a more general understanding of the dynamics of middleman minorities, all these variables have to be assessed and weighed. Whether a group develops into a middleman minority, rather than a subordinate minority, can be predicted by the presence and strength of particular variables, as can the probable persistence of the middleman form over time. Once established, the cohesion of the middleman community will promote economic concentration and economic concentration will 'feed back' to enhance communal solidarity. The initial hostility faced by the minority will not only restrict alternative economic opportunities but also strengthen cultural and social uniformity within the group as a mechanism of self-defence. This will aggravate the tendency for both majority and minority to view each other in terms of stereotypes and foster mutual distrust.

Such a situation is potentially very dangerous as the middleman minority is concentrated in occupations defined by the majority as 'exploitative' or 'deviant', and so they can easily be made scapegoats by politicians wishing to divert attention away from general economic ills or other political problems. They can also be the targets of those wishing to plunder their wealth or to remove them as economic competitors. In this way they can be the victims of both 'rational' and irrational persecution. It is true that middleman minorities need not necessarily develop in this direction, and some groups can be gradually integrated, or even assimilated, into the wider society after a certain period of time. However, in many cases, they are literally 'hostage groups' (Kuper, 1981:74) subject to savage attacks, expulsions and even genocidal massacres. The final outcome will depend on the structure and balance of power within the society, and, for some groups, on questions of international relations.

The case of middleman minorities is particularly interesting for the way in which it highlights the interconnections between race relations and power relations in several different societies. While some of the best examples of this type of minority group formation can be found in the plural societies of the Third World, in Africa, the Caribbean and Asia (H. Kuper, 1969:247–82; Nicholls, 1981), and are frequently a legacy of colonial policies, there are numerous other cases in advanced industrial settings. Both in the last century and in more recent times, Chinese, Japanese, Indian, Jewish and Arab middleman groups have established themselves in the United States, Canada, Britain and Australia (Bonacich & Modell, 1980; Chan, 1982; Curson & Curson, 1982; Zenner, 1982). The expulsion of the Ugandan Asians by Idi Amin in 1972, and their resettlement in Britain, Canada and other industrial societies, shows how the middleman form can not only persist after decolonization (with its susceptibility to nationalist and demagogic hostility), but also the manner in which these communities can be reconstituted in totally different societies (Pereira, Adams & Bristow, 1978).[5]

So far in this chapter I have discussed the general impact of social change on race and ethnic relations, with particular emphasis on the consequences for groups living in plural societies. As a result of the fragility of the state in so many ex-colonial, Third World countries, ethnic and racial conflict has frequently escalated into military violence and warfare (Enloe, 1980). This is hardly surprising in view of the arbitrary manner in which the colonial powers divided up the African continent, the Middle East and Asia with scant regard to ethnic, cultural and linguistic divisions (Stone, 1982). However, in recent years, and particularly since the 1960s, there have been a number of violent eruptions in Western industrial states, calling attention to the fact that these societies also have deep-seated racial, ethnic and national divisions. Indeed, it has been claimed by many scholars that there has been an 'ethnic revival' in the modern world, but this assertion must be examined and interpreted with considerable caution (Smith, 1981b).

First of all, a distinction needs to be drawn between two different types of ethnic mobilization. The resurgence of ethnicity in the United States among the newer European immigrant groups – the so-called 'white ethnics' – took place at much the same time as the revival of many ethno-national groups in Europe, Canada and other parts of the world. This coincidence in time, however, does not mean that these two developments are part of the same broad process (Connor, 1980:355–9). A greater sense of group identity and political awareness among Irish, Italian, Polish, Greek and Slavic groups in America had been noted by many observers, including both serious scholars and popular writers (Glazer & Moynihan, 1970; Greeley, 1974; Novak, 1971). The true significance of this ethnic resurgence has been the subject of enormous debate. Assessing the state of ethnic relations in New York City in 1970, Glazer and Moynihan suggested that the increased salience of ethnic identity during the decade of the 1960s could be attributed to several factors. These included: a decline in the prestige of traditional working-class occupational roles; the displacement of international events by domestic issues as a focus for ethnic identification; and a relative decline in religion as a source of primary group loyalty (Glazer & Moynihan, 1970:xxxi–xlii). Modifying their earlier prediction that religion and race were taking over from ethnicity as the prime bases of American group life, they considered that, by the end of the decade, ethnicity and race were the more important variables.

Some critics raised a further question about the nature of this heightened sense of ethnic attachment: was the resurgence of ethnicity simply a disguised form of racism? There can be little doubt that the white ethnic revival was in some measure a reaction to the black civil rights struggles of the 1950s and 1960s. The apparent success of the various black movements in their attempts to secure a fairer share of the resources of American society was seen as a particular threat to the white ethnic groups. Those most affected by the measures designed to compensate for racial disadvantage – busing schemes, open housing legislation and affirmative action policies in employment – were not the white liberals, who were the most vociferous allies of the black civil rights leaders, but the white ethnics. It was these 'hard hats' who were disproportionately represented in the public schools, poorer suburbs and blue collar occupations. Competition, as I have already noted, is an important ingredient of racial conflict, and the intensity of conflict is most keenly felt on the margins between poorer whites and upwardly mobile blacks, rather than between the rich and the poor. Whether white ethnic identification was a product of racism, a defence of interests and privileges, or a genuine search for cultural identity and cultural preservation is a complex matter. There is no reason why it should not have been a result of all three factors as Glazer and Moynihan concluded:

> We believe the conflicts . . . involve a mixture of *interests*: the defense of specific occupations, jobs, income and property; of *ethnicity*: the attachment to a specific group and its patterns; and of *racism*: the American (though not only American) dislike and fear of the racial other, in America's case in particular compounded by the heritage of slavery and the forcible placing of Negroes into a less than human position. (1970:xli)

The interpretation of the meaning of white ethnicity had been the subject of intense controversy throughout the 1970s. Some social scientists questioned the claim that there had been a revival at all, in the sense that ethnic community life had become more cohesive and meaningful. The reason why there had appeared to be an ethnic resurgence could be attributed to two main factors. Firstly, the upward social mobility of third and fourth generation white ethnics had made them more visible as leading politicians, academics and media personalities. So what appeared to be a greater ethnic assertiveness was, in reality, an index of the greater *assimilation* of these groups into the mainstream of American society. Secondly, the actual character of ethnicity had changed, so that for these later generations it was more a source of identity than a question of membership in a tightly knit social community.

This was, in Herbert Gans's phrase, 'symbolic ethnicity' (1979:1–20), and, as the mass media were better able to communicate symbols than the ethnic cultures and organizations of earlier generations, it was not surprising that the ethnic shadow could be mistaken for the ethnic substance. Claims that there was still significant ethnic discrimination, unlike the evidence for the persistence of institutional racism, carried little plausibility. Intermarriage rates, although not an entirely unambiguous index, seemed to point towards a greater degree of ethnic mixing (Alba, 1976; 1985a). Thus Gans could argue that 'the visibility of symbolic ethnicity provides further support for the existence of an ethnic revival, but what appears to be a revival is probably the emergence of a new form of acculturation and assimilation that is taking place under the gaze of the rest of society' (1979:12).

Other scholars have been even more dismissive of the whole ethnic issue. Stephen Steinberg has attacked the claims of the 'new pluralists' as an ethnic myth, an attempt to resurrect an 'iron law of ethnicity', thereby exaggerating the role of culture at the expense of more crucial social structural and, particularly, class factors. Although he concedes that ethnicity may play some causal role in the development of American society, he insists that it must also be seen as closely interrelated with material variables (1981:87). In general, ethnic conflict is simply a 'surface manifestation' of class conflict and ethnic barriers an alternative form of class barriers (ibid, 258). So while, in theory, Steinberg allows for cultural variables, in practice he sees them as almost entirely subservient to economic forces.

In the last chapter, I pointed to the danger of this approach: that ethnicity cannot be collapsed into class no matter how important the material dimension may be on many occasions. If indeed there has been an ethnic revival, economic factors alone cannot explain why mobilization should have assumed an ethnic rather than a class form. Nevertheless, by the early 1980s, the strength of the white ethnic movement appeared to have subsided, and those who had regarded it as little more than a minor interruption on the long path towards the assimilation of all white American groups seemed to have made the more convincing argument. The position of the racial minorities, blacks, Hispanics and American Indians, remained a rather different question.[6]

The second major aspect of the 'ethnic revival' concerned

the growth of the ethno-national movements on a worldwide scale. Unlike the white ethnics of North America, these groups were not a product of relatively recent immigration but were long-settled, teritorial groups whose demands ranged from regional autonomy and cultural rights to separate statehood. What caught most observers by surprise was the prevalence of these movements in advanced industrial societies, and particularly their concentration in the old-established states of Western Europe. The widespread assumption that European society had evolved beyond the point where ethnic mobilization would pose a threat to the integrity of the state was shattered by the simultaneous outbreak of nationalist demands throughout the continent. This was yet another example of the belief discussed at the beginning of the chapter that 'modernization' (industrialization, urbanization etc. necessarily diminishes ethnic allegiances.

What were the factors behind the revival of ethno-nationalism? Some scholars pointed to a connection between the political changes which had brought about the end of the European empires and the post-imperial fragmentation of the metropolitan societies. Direct confirmation of this hypothesis could be found in the statements by leaders of the Scottish National Party who conceded that Union with England might have been worthwhile when there was a worldwide empire to exploit, but to be the junior partner of one of the weaker European economies was a very different proposition. Other connections between the end of imperialism and growing European nationalism could take a variety of forms. The case of Corsica is one such example, where the termination of the Algerian war not only ended the migration of islanders to France's North African colony, but also resulted in the influx of former French settlers, the *pieds noirs* as the Corsicans referred to them, who had been 'repatriated' after independence (Kofman, 1982:300–12). Competition between these groups, who had managed with government assistance to become modern agriculturalists, and the less successful indigenous farming community, became one source of local resentment that increased support for Corsican autonomist movements.

The end of empire was only one factor behind the growth of European nationalist movements. Many other influences could be linked to some of the unanticipated consequences of modernization (Burgess, 1978:280). Both scholars and politicians have stressed the role of centralization, ironically viewed by many as an index of the strength and unity of the state, as a major cause of nationalist resentment. One notable fact about many European separatist movements has been their concentration in the highly centralized states of Britain, France and Spain. While in countries like Italy and Germany, the least centralized and historically among the newer states of Europe, the surge of rediscovered nationalism has had its least impact. In Italy, central government has tended to be weak as a legacy of late unification combined with a strong tradition of municipal and regional independence. In the German case, decentralization was a product of deliberate policy implemented at the end of the Second World War as a measure to impede the resurgence of militant German nationalism. However, while centralization might be one factor causing ethnic mobilization, it is not the only relevant variable. For both Switzerland, with its classic decentralized political structure of cantons, and federal Canada have been faced with the demands of ethnic minorities, respectively the French-speaking Jurassians and the Québécois (Steiner & Obler, 1977:324–42; Richmond, 1984).

It is the size and effectiveness of the traditional European state that some scholars have suggested is a more important factor. These states were geared to the demands and realities of the last century and have become, it is argued, increasingly anachronistic in the twentieth century. On the one hand, they are too small to deal effectively with the demands of global defence or to curb the economic strength of the multinational corporations. On the other hand, they are too large and remote to handle local community and regional matters with sensitivity, such as education and language policy, welfare, policing and cultural affairs. Thus they have fallen between two stools, losing functions to supranational organizations like the EEC and NATO, and hence their rationale and legitimacy in the eyes of many nationalist groups. At the same time, they have failed to offset the consequences of rapid social change which have threatened communal solidarity and confused individual identity – the familiar problems of industrial alienation and urban *anomie*. The attempt to reinstate cultural and linguistic traditions, particularly where these have been the subject of neglect or outright hostility by central governments, is one possible response to these pressures.

No one could deny that economic factors are also involved and closely interrelated with these major trends promoting ethno-national movements. There is quite clearly an instrumental side to what is often seen as an expressive or cultural phenomenon, and, by some, even as the persistence of a 'primordial' sense of attachment. The real question is the nature of the link between economic forces and regional movements, for it is by no means a simple relationship between absolute economic deprivation and ethnic discontent. While many ethno-national movements develop in areas with depressed economies and low income levels, others, such as those of the Basques and the Catalans in Spain, have emerged in areas of relative prosperity, even though the nationalists define their situation as one of exploitation (Heiberg, 1975:169–93; Llobera, 1983:332–50). It is a sense of *relative* deprivation which is the crucial determinant of social action: Catalan and Basque leaders have argued that the government in Madrid is draining off wealth from their regions for the benefit of the Castilian power centre. Similarly, the sudden discovery of new wealth, such as oil fields or mineral deposits, can also generate a sense of deprivation and contribute to the growth of nationalist movements. The link between North Sea oil discoveries and Scottish nationalism (Esman, 1977:251–86), and, in the Third World, between similar sources of wealth and separatist movements in Biafra, Katanga and Cabinda,[7] suggests that relative deprivation experienced by comparatively prosperous regions, particularly where they are denied commensurate political power, may stimulate violent ethnic conflict and even precipitate civil wars.

It is these types of situation that suggest reservations about Michael Hechter's influential 'internal colonialism' model of ethnic mobilization (Hechter, 1975). In fact, Hechter himself has modified and extended his earlier formulation of these ideas in the light of the considerable controversy they have provoked (Hechter & Levi, 1979:26–74; Smith, 1981b:29–37). The original internal colonialism thesis was applied to British national development over the long historical period from the sixteenth century until the 1960s. It attempted to explain the persistence of nationalist feeling in the Celtic fringe of Ireland, Scotland and Wales by associating it with an uneven process of industrialization. An initial advantage held by a core region – in this case England – resulted in an unequal distribution of power and resources which was accentuated as industrialization proceeded. The core economy became richer at the expense of unbalanced and dependent peripheral economic regions. Since these coincided with cultural differences, peripheral ethnic groups developed a strong sense of separate nationhood and started to demand greater autonomy and independence.

While this analysis gives a more plausible account of the persistence of nationalism than crude modernization theories, it is deficient in a number of crucial respects. It fails to distinguish between important divisions within the so-called 'cores' and 'peripheries' (McRoberts, 1979:293–318); it cannot account for the nationalism found in relatively prosperous regions; and it gives little explanation for the timing of nationalist revivals. In order to explain these facts, it is necessary to move away from the 'internal colonialism' (or reactive) model towards what have been called 'competitive' models (Beer, 1979:201–33; Mughan & McAllister, 1981:189–204; Olzak, 1982:253–75). Perhaps the clearest demonstration of this approach is provided by Anthony Mughan in his attempt to develop a theory of ethnic conflict out of the interaction between modernization, a sense of relative deprivation, and the regional distribution of power resources (Mughan, 1979). It is argued that the politicisation of ethnic divisions results from a sense of relative deprivation, which is, in its turn, generated by the uneven distribution of the benefits of modernization among ethnic groups. The relative deprivation hypothesis outlines a necessary but not a sufficient condition for political conflict between groups because it emphasizes the motivational side of conflict without considering the actual possibilities for achieving the desired change. It is important, therefore, to focus on the distribution of power resources, and particularly shifts in the balance of power, during the modernization process. Mughan illustrates his argument with reference to the Belgian, British, Canadian and Nigerian experiences of ethnic conflict.

The reason why modernization took so long to precipitate ethnic conflict in the first three cases was because it failed to disturb the ethnic status quo consolidated in the early stages of industrial growth. Subordinate ethnic groups came to possess more power resources but not at the expense of the dominant ethnic group, so the balance of political power remained unaltered. This general situation persisted until the end of the Second World War. By contrast, ethnic conflict came to dominate the political life of many Third World states after independence because modernization did not systematically favour one particular ethnic group. The amorphous distribution of power resources in Nigeria, for example, invited political conflict as the Ibos sought self-determination against the numerically superior Northerners. Thus, 'ethnic relations in the former countries were characterized by cumulative status discrepancies for a long time after the start of the modernization process, while in Nigeria they were characterized by politically volatile status inconsistencies right from the time of the departure of the colonial power' (1979:12).

This approach adds an important element to our understanding of the development of ethnic conflict by not only stressing regional imbalances in resources resulting in a sense of relative deprivation, but also the way in which this change in the balance of power can lead to a competitive struggle. This, in turn, produces ethnic mobilization and demands for national self-determination. The value of this model is that it can be as easily applied to the Third World as to the ethnic resurgence in industrialized states. Indeed, attempts to industrialize in the Third World in the space of a short period of time are likely to accentuate these strains, both because of the rapidity of social change and also as a result of the method of industrialization through centralized political planning.

The analysis of ethnic movements also requires some consideration of the policies pursued by central governments: how they manage to exploit divisions in the nationalist movements; whether government elites are perceptive enough to grant concessions at a sufficiently early stage to undermine the appeals of separatism; and whether they have the military capacity to suppress violent attempts to secure nationalist goals.[8] It should be clear that no one factor or theory can provide a comprehensive explanation for the resurgence of ethnic nationalism. A complex causal chain is usually involved combining several unanticipated consequences of modernization: the strains of over-centralization and bureaucracy; the emergence of supra-state organizations in certain important spheres; the attractions of ethnic movements as an antidote to urban *anomie* and industrial alienation; and the role of uneven economic development producing a sense of relative deprivation. All these factors have been at work behind the current revival of the 'stateless nations' in the industrialized world, and are variables relevant to the rise of demands for ethnic self-determination in the Third World.

What I have attempted to illustrate in this chapter is the manner in which social change, and particularly what is generally called 'modernization', can create, as much as it can destroy, a sense of racial and ethnic identity. The outcome will depend on the way in which the forces of social change affect the balance of *power* between the various ethnic and racial groups in society.

5 Race relations and social institutions

The emphasis that I have placed on the importance of power in determining the origin and development of race and ethnic relations can also be applied to an understanding of how race relations operate throughout the whole range of major social institutions. This chapter considers the manner in which patterns of race and ethnic relations in various societies are reflected in the structure and functioning of their key institutions. I will start with the most basic and crucial social institution, the family, and then analyse how policies designed to influence the nature of race and ethnic relations affect education, housing, employment, politics, law enforcement and the military structure of the state. As these institutions are enormously complicated, permeating every conceivable aspect of social life, I will be highly selective and consider only certain problems that particularly highlight the effect of power on group relations.

The great French sociologist and historian, Alexis de Tocqueville, once observed that the acid test of whether a society had eradicated its major social divisions lay in its marriage customs (1966:108). What Tocqueville proposed as a measure for the rigidity of all systems of social stratification is particularly relevant in the case of racial and ethnic stratification. Most racial and ethnic groups exhibit a tendency towards endogamy – marriages being generally confined to within the group – although how the 'group' is defined may vary considerably. Of all relationships between groups intermarriage is generally the last barrier to be breached. In the United States, this can be seen in the results produced by the Bogardus social distance test, a classic scale developed to measure attitudes concerning intergroup relations in which respondents are asked to express opinions about the levels of contact and association they would be prepared to sustain with members of different groups (Bogardus, 1928; 1958). The acceptance of an individual of another ethnic or racial group as a fellow citizen, as a colleague or as a neighbour, rarely evokes the same degree of resistance as acceptance 'as a close relation by marriage'. This is hardly surprising since intermarriage will, in general, result in a breakdown in group boundaries. While the acceptable levels of interracial association appear to follow a fairly stable pattern, this does not imply that attitudes towards intermarriage are similar among all groups or in all societies. Considerable variations occur both in different cultures and from one historical period to another.

One of the most rigid forms of group boundary maintenance can be found in the Indian caste system, although the rules of inter- and intragroup marriage are exceptionally complicated (Srinivas, 1969:265–72). Major caste groups are subdivided into in-marrying *jatis* which are further broken down into both endogamous and exogamous *gotras*. As Philip Mason explains:

It is essential to marry within the *jati*, but many *jatis* are divided into *gotras* or clans, which are exogamous; a man must marry a woman from a *gotra* not his own, and sometimes, though not always, from a *gotra* counting as lower than his own. (1970:141)

This classic pattern of rigid group boundaries, involving strict rules of endogamy supported by an ideology of ritual pollution, has led some social scientists to use the term *caste* outside the Indian context (Berreman, 1960:120–7). Others have objected strongly to this practice arguing that it is totally misleading to apply the term to any system unless it is supported by a set of beliefs in which all groups, both the dominant and the subordinate, accept a basic premise of inequality (Dumont, 1970:265–94). They would assert that it is inappropriate to use the concept of caste when analysing patterns of racial stratification which, like the chattel slavery of the

Southern states of America and the Caribbean, was not accepted by the slaves as a legitimate social order.[1]

Nevertheless, a strict prohibition against interracial marriage existed in the South during the slave era, but this did not prevent interracial sexual relationships from taking place on an extensive scale. In fact, such miscegenation was probably *more* common under slavery than after emancipation, although these unions were almost entirely of a particular kind which reflected the power structure of the slave plantation: between the dominant white males and the subordinate black females.[2] What happens to the offspring of these relationships is particularly interesting and tells us a lot about the nature of the society involved. It will depend on a number of factors such as the sex ratio in the dominant group; the political and economic value of creating intermediate groups between dominant and subordinate sections of the society; cultural and religious attitudes towards sex and marriage; and the ethnic diversity of the subordinate groups.

Such influences on the early history of interracial contact and subordination resulted, depending on their precise combination and intensity, in several different patterns. In the North American case, the children born from miscegenation were assigned to membership of a single subordinate racial category: any amount of 'black' ancestry causing individuals to be classed as 'black', unless, of course, they are able to disguise this fact by 'passing' as 'white'. By way of contrast, the Cape Coloureds of South Africa have developed as a distinct intermediate group (despite their very diverse origins) between the dominant white minority and the subordinate black majority (Dickie-Clark, 1966; Ross, 1983). In Brazil, miscegenation has resulted in a colour continuum, with no specific intermediate groups as such, but a whole spectrum of finely differentiated statuses, in which colour and ancestry are only elements in a total package of characteristics that determine an individual's position in society. Finally, in Mexico, the mestizos, the mixed group, have emerged as the dominant political force, combining the cultural ideal and the social norm. Thus the interplay between sexual and political relations can result in very different outcomes.

Despite emancipation, interracial marriage remained illegal in many American states, particularly in the South and West, until the Supreme Court finally declared such barriers to intermarriage unconstitutional in 1967 (Heer, 1980:514). Interracial marriages still remain a small but growing proportion of intergroup marriages, estimated at less than one per cent of the total US marriages in 1970 (ibid, 518–19). But if the number of interracial marriages in the United States is small, the trend in interethnic marriages, between individuals from different religious and national origin backgrounds, has increased much more dramatically. A pioneering study by Ruby Kennedy based on marriage records in New Haven, Connecticut between 1870 and 1950, using the somewhat unreliable index of surnames to determine nationality groups, revealed a pattern of growing intermarriage between brides and grooms of different national origins. However, there was little religious intermarriage between Protestants, Catholics and Jews. This led the author to propose a 'triple melting pot' hypothesis: a consolidation of individuals from diverse national backgrounds into three major religious groups (Kennedy, 1944; 1952).

The conclusions of this study have been questioned from a number of different perspectives, both on the grounds that New Haven was hardly typical of the rest of the United States (Heer, 1980:516–17), and also that the study itself contained a series of methodological flaws. On replicating the research, Ceri Peach concluded:

Kennedy's triple religious-national melting pot did not exist . . . a racial-ethnic division of society into Black, Jewish and white Gentile would be a more accurate description of the New Haven data than Kennedy's Protestant, Catholic and Jewish melting pots. (1980:15–16)

Data on interreligious marriages are always complicated by a considerable degree of conversion which makes it appear that the number of individuals from different religious backgrounds marrying one another is lower than the true figure. One study suggested that more than fifty-seven per cent of couples involved in Protestant-Catholic marriages in Detroit changed from an original situation of religious difference to a religiously homogeneous relationship at the time of their marriage.[3] As a result of this and other recent research studies, David Heer argues:

> Rather than describing the United States as a triple melting pot in which each of the three major religious groups maintains its identity through low rates of intermarriage, it would be more accurate to dub the United States a double melting pot in which the major barrier is between blacks and all others. (1980:521)

Once again, marriage patterns would appear to reflect the power structure of American society where racial divisions are far more significant in determining life styles and life chances than either ethnic or religious barriers.

Part of this can be explained in terms of the relative economic position of different minority groups. In industrial societies generally, people tend to select marriage partners from a similar socio-economic background to their own. Thus the greater the economic equality between ethnic and racial groups, the greater the probability that eligible partners will emerge from minority groups and this should eventually lead to an increase in the rates of intermarriage. However, decisions to marry are influenced by a whole range of factors and may have a differential impact according to the sex of the person involved. As Yochanan Peres and Ruth Schrift observe: 'economic gains or hazards, parental disapproval, breaking previous social ties and forming new ones – all of these could affect men and women differently' (Peres & Schrift, 1978:428). Of course, economic factors alone are an incomplete explanation of such a complex social process, and general levels of ethnocentrism in society, as well as the overall ratio of the sexes, can also have a major influence on the rate of intermarriage.

More detailed research on the relationships between inter-marriage and interethnic relations needs to be explored against evidence derived from cross-national data. Peres and Schrift have attempted to test a number of basic hypotheses concerned with probable frequency of intermarriage using data gathered from the United States, Israel and South Africa. Although certain generalizations do seem to be confirmed, comparisons of this kind pose many problems because of the enormous variations in the context in which intermarriage occurs. For example, the obvious factor of the size of various ethnic groups in a given society must also be controlled in any comparison since it will affect the availability of eligible partners. Bearing these qualifications in mind, it is reasonable to assume that the ratio of expected (if mates were selected at random) to actual intermarriages will be strongly influenced by the relative economic status of the various ethnic and racial groups. Other things being equal, the greater the equality in resource dis-tribution among ethnic groups, the greater the penetration of members of minority groups into positions where they become eligible partners for members of the dominant group, and this will ultimately result in increased rates of intermarriage. Similarly, within groups it is the lower status members of the dominant group and the higher status members of minorities who are more likely to intermarry, as there is a greater prob-ability that their economic situations will overlap.

A second major dimension influencing the rate of intermar-riage is the level of group ethnocentrism in a particular soci-ety. Ethnic inequality and ethnocentrism are linked in com-plex ways since the lowest stratum of a dominant group, fearing competition, is often highly ethnocentric (as my pre-vious discussion of the 'split labour' market and 'labour aristo-cracy' theories suggests) and, therefore, the degree of econo-mic compatibility may well be submerged by the extent of differential class ethnocentrism. It may then be necessary for upwardly mobile members of minority groups to be ex-ceptionally mobile in educational and economic terms in order to leapfrog this 'barrier group' and find potential majority group partners from the less intolerant, higher status sections of the dominant community. As Peres and Schrift remark: 'when ethnocentrism is intense, especially among the relatively low class groups, it takes a considerable increase in interethnic equality to produce a significant rise in intermarriage' (1978:430).

Changes in levels of ethnic inequality and degrees of ethnocentrism do not simply affect the incidence of inter-marriage, but also the likely pattern. There has been a long-recognized tendency for hypergamy to be more common than hypogamy: that minority group women are more likely to marry men of a higher social status, than minority men to be involved in intermarriages (Davis, 1941; Merton, 1941). One explanation for this is the fact that in most societies the status of a family is determined to a greater extent by the status of the husband than by that of the wife. As a result, women have more to gain, and correspondingly more to lose, by marrying a man of a higher or lower status than their own, while for a male this is a less pressing factor. A reduction in ethnic inequality should result in an increase in the number of minority males involved in intermarriages, while a reduction in general ethnocentrism should increase the proportion of majority females partici-pating in mixed marriages.

In general, comparative studies support the proposition that intermarriages increase with greater ethnic equality and decreased ethnocentrism. However, data derived from the Israeli experience suggest that a point is reached when intermarriage passes a threshold and becomes a major force promoting ethnic in-tegration. This increase in the incidence of intermarriage may then start to react on its pattern. For when the ratio of mixed marriages to all marriages becomes a substantial figure, then a significant discrepancy in the pattern of male and female marriages would create a large number of single men and women. It would appear, if the Israeli example is of any guidance, that these individuals tend to overcome their ethnocentric scruples in order to increase the field of choice of eligible marriage partners. In this way, intermarriage can become a major force breaking down ethnic boundaries, although in most societies it is as much a consequence as a cause of reduced prejudice and discrimination.

Levels of intermarriage are one major indication of the relative power of ethnic and racial groups. This is because the family is a crucial institution in society bound up with the ownership and transfer of property, skills and wealth. It also plays a key role in the process of socialization, how the young learn both the central values and the instrumental skills necessary to survive in society. In most complex societies it is not only the family that caters for these needs as specialized educational institutions have been developed to fulfil these functions.

However, the educational system does not simply impart 'knowledge' in terms of skills and values, it also occupies a strategic position in the processes of social selection and social control. Just as educational institutions and policies have assumed a central place in the debate about general inequality, so they are often seen as a crucial arena in which the struggle for racial and ethnic equality is fought out. This has been recognized under many different types of social and political regimes: most plantation masters were determined to prevent their slaves from learning to read or write, appreciating the force of the old maxim that 'knowledge is power'. The fact that the most spectacular rebellions against slavery in the South were often led by educated slaves, like Nat Turner, suggests that they were right! A similar recognition can be found in Dr Verwoerd's[4] efforts to build a system of inferior and elementary 'Bantu education' for the African majority in South Africa – a clear case, as one of its many critics observed, of 'education for barbarism' (Stone, 1973:70–3).

In order to illustrate the way in which education and race relations have become increasingly interrelated in the contemporary world, I will select two sets of issues that have been at the centre of debate in recent years. These are the questions of school busing and the arguments over the value and relevance of multicultural and bilingual curricula. Both issues concern power and the distribution of educational resources, and while busing has received most attention in relation to school integration in the USA, it has been by no means confined to North American education, either as a policy or as a theoretical solution to the problem of educational inequality. The debate on the content and style of teaching, as reflected in multiculturalism and bilingualism,[5] is definitely a major international issue which is explicitly relevant to many different societies (Bullivant, 1981; 1982).

The question of busing, the physical transfer of students from one school to another in order to achieve a greater measure of racial integration, emerged as an important instrument of American race relations policy during the 1960s and 1970s. It produced an enormous degree of controversy and revealed bitter racial hostility, with both educational specialists and ordinary members of the public sharply divided about its wisdom and effectiveness. The main objectives of school desegregation – a policy made possible by the 1954 *Brown versus the Board of Education* decision of the Supreme Court which declared that racially segregated schools violated black children's constitutional rights – appear deceptively simple. The chief aims of desegregation include: (i) to end the isolation of racial and ethnic groups in particular schools (ii) to increase tolerance and understanding among children and adults of all racial and ethnic groups (iii) to improve the academic performance of low achievers (iv) to increase the self-concept and aspirations among minorities (v) and to promote racial equality by increasing minority access to further education, higher status jobs and hence better incomes (Hawley, 1981:146). In sum, racial integration in American schools was designed as part of a strategy to reduce racial disadvantage, not merely in education but throughout the whole of the society. The question of implementing this policy, the extent to which busing was a necessary or sufficient condition for achieving it, and the conflicts between this goal and other constitutional rights (such as the guarantee of freedom of religion and its impact on private religious schools), have remained as persistent problems during the thirty years since the *Brown* decision.

What have been the actual consequences of this policy? The underlying theory behind school integration is that without these measures educational institutions will become divided between separate and inferior minority schools and those attended predominantly by the majority. Certainly the evidence suggests that integration policies during the 1960s and 1970s did reduce the levels of segregation, particularly between blacks and whites (Taeuber & Wilson, 1979). Ironically, the greatest progress was made in the South,[6] while in the Northern inner cities little meaningful desegregation was achieved. A major problem has been the movement of whites out of the city centres, a phenomenon generally known as 'white flight', into racially exclusive suburbs which has simply resulted in res-egregation, albeit with a different geographical pattern. Throughout the 1970s a major debate took place between those who felt that these unintended consequences of desegregation were more harmful than any benefits derived from the policy, and others who argued that to make the strategy more effective required certain modifications such as enlarging the catchment area of integration schemes to include the suburbs as well as the inner city (Pettigrew & Green, 1976; Coleman, 1976).

Even when this process has not occurred, other complications have arisen, leading to what Thomas Pettigrew has called 'mere desegregation' (Pettigrew, 1971 in 1977:387). For although schools may have achieved an integrated enrolment, a number of developments within these nominally mixed schools have tended to perpetuate racial disadvantage. This can result from a higher 'drop out' rate among minority students; the streaming (or 'tracking' to use the North American term) of children into different 'ability' groups which tends to reproduce any initial differences in racial achievement within the institution; classifying minority students as 'educationally subnormal' with-out any regard to ethnocentric biases in this labelling (Tomlinson, 1981); or simply racial prejudice among the teaching staff which may take many subtle forms, including differences in expectations which often play a crucial part in motivating students.

It is clear that the effects of integration depend on the

context and manner in which such programmes are implemented. The attitudes of teachers, the commitment of administrators, and the influence of parents are all important factors. Some settings have been conspicuously more successful than others. It has been suggested that there is a minimum ratio of minority to majority students, estimated very roughly at between ten and twenty per cent, necessary to prevent the former from feeling threatened and isolated, thereby undermining their self-esteem and sense of identity which are often felt to be associated with academic achievement. Desegregation at an early age, as well as a measure of stability in the educational environment, are other important elements that seem to affect the success or failure of these policies.

Whether integration can be achieved in the first place also depends on a broad range of factors. This is, perhaps, best illustrated by the remarkable contrast in the experience of the North and South since the era of court-ordered desegregation. Such legal remedies have helped to remove the dual education system in the South and have had greater long-term success than similar policies applied to major Northern metropolitan areas. The reasons behind these regional disparities need to be carefully analysed, particularly since this result was so generally unanticipated (Orfield, 1978). When Federal paratroopers were needed to protect nine black children wishing to attend a previously all-white high school in Little Rock, Arkansas during 1957, few observers expected that integrated education would be peacefully accepted in the South within a generation. In a fascinating reversal of previous traditions, it was the formerly 'liberal' Boston that was to become the symbol of racial anta gonism during the 1970s precisely over the issue of school busing. The change in the South was genuinely remarkable since, in the early 1960s, ninety-nine out of every hundred black children attended all-black schools. In the mid-1970s, only fourteen per cent of black children still attended such schools and, by the end of the decade, desegregated schooling had ceased to be a major issue in Southern politics. In fact, nearly all the anti-busing motions in Congress were initiated by Northern members of the House or the Senate (Orfield, 1981:21).

What explanation can be given for this development that seemed to run counter to the previous tide of American race relations? The South had a number of advantages once the initial opposition to racially integrated schools had been overcome. Southern cities were smaller and had nothing to match the vast urban complexes of New York, Chicago or Los Angeles. Recent demographic trends had created a more balanced pattern of black/white residence, with a substantial inflow of whites matched by an equally significant exodus of blacks. Furthermore, the North had to contend with a far more diversified set of ethnic and religious divisions among its school population. With the notable exceptions of Texas and southern Florida, the South had no large Hispanic enrolments which required complicated, three-way desegregation plans. Generally, the South lacked the familiar pattern of declining inner cities and new suburban development that proved to be a major hurdle in the path of Northern desegregation plans (Yarmolinsky, Liebman & Schelling, 1981). Northern whites intent on avoiding integrated schools had more opportunities to side-step the consequences of mandatory busing by moving to all-white suburbs or retreating to predominantly white private or religious schools.

This is an excellent illustration of the need to consider the overall power balance when framing policies to create a greater measure of racial and ethnic equality. It is essential to recognize not merely the strength of central government resolve, nor simply the various minority reactions to racial oppression, but also the ability of majorities and dominant minorities to adapt to changed circumstances. White power and black power, the strength and resources of minorities and majorities are related dialectically, so that what is won in the battle for school integration may well be lost in the war against racial inequality. It is a recognition of this dilemma that has caused some of the early advocates of school integration to be highly critical of busing which they now view as being far too crude an instrument to perform successfully one of the most delicate operations in intergroup relations (Coleman, 1966; 1981). These sociologists favour various forms of incentives that would produce a greater measure of integration through consent, rather than trying to enforce a system of racially mixed schools by legal means (Coleman, 1981:182–93). Other social scientists regard such proposals as a totally inadequate response to the challenge of racial inequality in education, which might also inadvertently serve to legitimize racial segregation, and argue in favour of more stringently enforced, broadly based, metropolitan approaches to busing and integration (Pettigrew, 1981:161–81).

While busing has formed a major part in American race relations policy, it was never adopted to any significant extent in Britain. This was partly a result of the reluctance to pursue racially explicit policies which became the hallmark of official British approaches towards race relations until the 1970s (Kirp, 1979). In fact, dispersal policies were opposed on the grounds that they were 'racist', a remarkably different interpretation from that found in the United States. The Race Relations Board, the body responsible for enforcing the law on racial equality, actually took legal action to prevent a local education authority from continuing the practice in 1976. In Britain busing received very little support from any group:

> It was attacked from every quarter: liberals advocating community education argued that it militated against parental involvement in schooling and undermined community stability; West Indian and Asian pressure groups, along with sectors of the Left, viewed the policy as discriminatory and a concession to racist sentiment (reinforcing the popular stereotype of Asian and West Indian students as educational 'problems', and singling them out, rather than whites, for busing); and neo-fascist groups claimed that it constituted 'discrimination in reverse'. (Carrington, 1981:295)

Despite these interesting transatlantic contrasts, both Britain and the United States were involved in a broad debate about the nature of the school curriculum which, some would argue, had just as significant an effect on both the climate of race relations, and on the levels of achievement of minority groups, as the actual racial and ethnic composition of the school. This controversy has taken a number of forms: in the USA, it has centred on the merits and defects associated with black studies programmes and bilingual education; in Britain, it has been concerned with the measures variously described as 'multi-ethnic', 'multi-cultural' or 'multi-racial' education (Fenton, 1982; Killian, 1983). The arguments concerning all these developments contain a number of related themes. There is the assumption that an education dominated by the majority's central values and world view (and, in a multilingual society, in the dominant language) will tend to undermine the self-esteem of minority students and this will place them at an educational disadvantage. It will have the effect of perpetuating negative stereotypes, of failing to make the majority sensitive to the cultural traditions and historical experience of minorities, and of creating learning and assessment problems for students whose mother tongue differs from the language of instruction of the classroom.[7]

Few would dispute the importance of removing explicit and implicit racist references in textbooks and teaching materials, avoiding the use of negative stereotypes, and correcting the ethnocentric biases usually found in traditional history courses. However, the value of bilingual education and the use of ethnic studies programmes are rather more complex issues. With language, it is by no means obvious who actually requires linguistic assistance and in what form it is best provided. In Britain, the education authorities have been more sensitive to the problems faced by Asian children than to those confronting West Indians. The need to provide supplementary language tuition to those whose home language is Urdu or Gujarati is more apparent than the difficulties faced by schooolchildren of West Indian origin using a 'dialect' or 'patois' form of English (Little & Willey, 1981:17–20). This may be one factor accounting for the different levels of academic achievement often found in studies of West Indian and Asian students. The issue of fully bilingual education in

Britain has only arisen in Wales,[8] and has been closely associated with the demands of the nationalist movement (Thomas & Williams, 1978:235–58).

In North America, the choice of the medium of instruction in schools has been a much more central issue. It has played a critical part in the dispute between Quebec and English-speaking Canada, while in the United States bilingualism has been generally associated with the large Spanish-speaking minorities, Chicanos, Puerto Ricans and, most recently, Cubans. However, the influential Supreme Court ruling in the case of *Lau versus Nichols* (1974) concerned the failure of the San Francisco public school district to provide adequate special educational assistance to non-English-speaking Chinese students (Baker & de Kanter, 1983:ix–xxi). The court declared:

There is no equality of treatment merely by providing students with the same facilities, textbooks, teachers and curriculum . . . for students who do not understand English are effectively foreclosed from any meaningful education . . . [which makes] a mockery of public education.

What the court did not specify was the particular means by which these disabilities were to be overcome, whether by supplementary English instruction, by tuition in the student's home language, or by some combination of the two.

Subsequent Federal policy, developed by the Office of Civil Rights and the Department of Education, has tended to encourage bilingualism, although the wisdom of this strategy has been challenged on several grounds (Epstein, 1977). While critics usually accept the claim that children from linguistic minorities may need special educational assistance, the type of aid that would be of most use is more debatable. The difficulties faced by these children may not be attributable to their dependence on a language other than English – it is quite possible that they are more skilled in English than in their home language – but to a deficiency in *both* languages. Recent studies suggest that class background and associated levels of poverty may account for much of the low achievement previously attributed to language problems, so that attempts to improve linguistic skills are at best only a partial solution. The effectiveness of bilingual education in purely academic terms is therefore questionable (Baker & de Kanter, 1983:33–86), as is the ability of school districts to provide qualified bilingual teachers, and the lack of reliable tests to assess children's language proficiency. There are also the complications that arise in areas where several minority languages are spoken.

However, for many advocates of bilingualism the policy is not just aimed at promoting educational achievement and a positive self-image, it also provides job protection for minority teachers and acts as 'an important weapon in strengthening the power of their own ethnic group' (Cohen, 1982:179). Mexican-American pressure groups have drawn up plans that segregate Hispanic schoolchildren in schools with bilingual programmes, producing a reversal of previous tactics in the battle against ethnic disadvantage. As Gaynor Cohen points out: 'segregation was no longer seen only in terms of a ploy by middle-class Anglos to maintain the low social status of minority groups, but as "the only way to preserve the ethnic culture of the barrio"' (ibid, 180). This strategy is based on a similar rationale to that of many of the black studies programmes and the dangers are obvious. Isolation from the majority can result in an erosion of financial support, so while the 'gilded ghetto' approach may appeal to community leaders and ethnic activists and, in theory, offer an opportunity for greater ethnic autonomy, in reality it can soon degenerate into educational apartheid. Qualifications in 'black' or 'Chicano' studies, or fluency in a minority language, may have little use in the employment market and may actually prove to be a liability when competing against individuals with technical or professional qualifications. Programmes designed to bolster a minority's self-esteem can well be misjudged when confidence is no longer the basic problem (Louden, 1981:153–74). Ironically, the very success of the black power movement may have made black studies increasingly redundant.

If this diagnosis is correct, then developing instrumental

skills, demanding a fair share of educational resources (if necessary by means of quotas), and removing discriminatory barriers in employment after education, become, the important priorities. It may be of greater value to direct multicultural studies towards students of majority background rather than to concentrate them on minorities, where such initiatives can become a substitute for basic education (Stone, 1981). Contemplating one's ethnic navel can be an expensive luxury in the hard world of group competition. Critics of multiculturalism as it is practised in Britain, Canada, the United States and Australia (Bullivant, 1981; Moodley, 1983) may be overstating the case when they dismiss it as trendy rhetoric, or even as a more sinister strategy for 'ethnic hegemony', but it is certainly right to emphasize the limitations of the education system confined as it is within the general power structure of society. As Brian Bullivant perceptively comments:

The school system and its associated teacher education cannot achieve anywhere near the degree of social change required through the curriculum. This in essence is the pluralist dilemma in education, but it is manifestly not being solved. (1981:226)

The connection between different institutions in society was clearly demonstrated by the impact of 'white flight' on American busing programmes. Discrimination in the housing market is, in part, a cause as well as a consequence of racial stratification in education. Housing inequality makes the search for greater equality in education more difficult and this, in turn, affects the pattern of racial disadvantage in employment. No serious policy aimed at eliminating racial and ethnic discrimination can consider one set of institutions in isolation from the others.

Although there are significant transatlantic differences in the mechanisms of housing allocation, the existence of widespread racial discrimination has been extensively documented in both Britain (Daniel, 1968; Smith, 1977)[9] and the United States (Taeuber & Taeuber, 1965; Farley, 1977). There have been many attempts to measure the extent and changes in residential segregation, particularly using the 'index of dissimilarity'. This measure gives an approximate indication of the spatial concentration or dispersal of racial and ethnic groups. Several major methodological problems are generally recognized with this index. For example, the scores, which range from 0 to 100 along a continuum (from complete dispersal to total segregation), vary considerably according to the size of the spatial unit used as a basis for calculation. The larger the unit the less sensitive the index becomes as a measure of local patterns of segregation. There is also a need to control for factors such as class before arriving at the conclusion that segregation is simply the product of racial discrimination.

Different racial and ethnic groups may have different preferences as far as the type of accommodation they desire, the particular amenities they require in their neighbourhood, and the extent to which they want to stay in close proximity to other members of their own group. However, there is much direct evidence to corroborate the pattern based on the statistical analysis of census data that racial minorities, blacks and Hispanics in America, and West Indians and Asians in Britain, suffer from discrimination in all areas of housing allocation. Investigations have convincingly demonstrated that estate agents and private vendors, landlords in both the private and public renting sector, as well as building societies, banks and other financial institutions providing loans for house purchase, have all operated in ways that have tended, either directly or indirectly, to discriminate against racial minorities.

These practices can be either crude or subtle. The imposition of what A. T. Carey called 'a colour tax', the additional rent demanded from black, as opposed to white, tenants, gives a precise measure of the cost of discrimination faced by West Indians in Britain during the 1950s (Carey, 1956:69–71). Less blatant examples can be seen in the activities of estate agents who only show black customers houses in predominantly black neighbourhoods, a practice referred to in the American literature as 'racial steering'. An even more insidious tech-

nique is that of 'blockbusting', provoking fears about the effect
on property values of a significant minority presence in a given
area, causing panic selling and a rapid change from an exclusively white to an all-black neighbourhood. The sole be-
neficiaries are the estate agents and property speculators who
can buy houses from the fleeing whites at a discount and sell
them back to blacks, who are eager to live in an 'integrated'
neighbourhood, at a premium. The net result is that the level
of segregation remains the same.

Local authority housing policy can also lead to racial discrimination in the allocation of the public housing stock. Rules
and regulations that appear to be universal, but place an excessive
emphasis on the length of local residence needed to qualify for
public housing, work against immigrants and more mobile
minorities whose actual housing needs may be greater than many
of the more permanently settled members of the indigenous
population. Selective slum clearance and development schemes
can be designed to avoid areas with a concentration of minority
group members; and biased assessments by housing officials may
result in minorities being offered the worst accommodation in the
least desirable council estates (Rex & Tomlinson, 1979:130–1).
Even though discrimination in housing has been illegal in Britain
and the United States since 1968, many recent studies show the
persistence of high indices of dissimilarity (Woods, 1979; van
Valey, 1977). It is easier to legislate against discrimination than to
enforce the law.

In an influential study of Birmingham during the 1960s,
John Rex and Robert Moore introduced the concept of 'housing classes' (1967:272–85) to emphasize the central part played
by the struggle over these resources in the evolution of inner
city race relations. The basic assumption behind the 'housing
class' concept is that in any urban area 'there is a stock of
housing of varying degrees of desirability to which different
groups of people having different characteristics have differing
degrees of access' (Rex & Tomlinson, 1979:127). Rex and
Moore's focus on housing, and particularly on the role of
multiple occupation in lodging houses located in the 'zone of

transition' (an idea adapted from the Chicago School's ecological model of race relations), has been the subject of much subsequent debate. While the special characteristics of Sparkbrook, the area on which the study was based, may have resulted in too much importance being attached to this particular mode of housing conflict, the concentration on the housing system itself reveals significant new dimensions of the urban power struggle between ethnic and racial groups. It is true that competition for housing need not always lead to conflict and can, under certain circumstances, result in interracial cooperation and alliances (Ward, 1979:204–22), but this tends to be the exception rather than the rule.

The question of access to a given housing stock is crucial and is by no means confined to a private market situation. In Britain, unlike the United States, there is a substantial public housing sector comprising almost thirty per cent, compared to less than two per cent of the total housing stock (McKay, 1977:40). The quality and the amenities of this public rented accommodation are by no means inferior, and are often far superior, to those found in the private sector. Influence over the administrative means of allocating public housing then becomes as critical an issue as that of preventing discrimination and disadvantage in the private housing market.

An important question to emerge from this discussion of the housing sector, and one analogous to the issue of busing in education, is whether policies should be aimed at dispersing minorities, so avoiding the geographical concentration of racial and ethnic communities. In North America, the overall picture of inner city, black and Hispanic ghettoes surrounded by a suburban noose of white affluent housing seems to have set in a fairly rigid pattern. Black suburban development, when it occurs, tends to result in exclusively black suburbs. As most potential white house purchasers prefer to avoid an integrated suburb, on the grounds that it will rapidly change its racial character, and as there is strong black demand to find decent suburban accommodation, the process becomes a self-fulfilling prophecy. Thus housing segregation will only be reduced by a combination of strategies: the rigorous enforcement of anti-discrimination legislation; changes in white attitudes and fears about the effect of minorities on property values and local amenities; and interracial cooperation at the community level to ensure the long-run stability of integrated neighbourhoods once they have been achieved. In Britain, with its more significant public sector, there is a need for housing authorities to adopt more sophisticated measures to develop ethnic and racial communities throughout the whole range of available properties, rather than pursuing crude attempts at dispersing individual families which not only entail illegal discrimination, but are unlikely to have any long-term success (Smith, 1977:302–8).

Segregation in housing also has an effect on the employment prospects of minority groups. Even without employment discrimination, an inability to live within a reasonable distance of one's work place adds significant travelling costs to the minority employee. Where public transport facilities are poor or non-existent, this may greatly reduce the choice of feasible jobs. As a growing number of new industries have moved out from inner city areas to suburban locations, this increasingly important development is another factor accounting for the higher rates of unemployment found among the minority work force. However, many forms of discrimination do persist in employment affecting both initial job opportunities and promotion. One common argument advanced to explain patterns of minority disadvantage in employment is that it is purely a result of inadequate skills and training. This raises Duncan's crucial question of whether the answer is to be found in 'inheritance of poverty or inheritance of race?' (Duncan, 1968). Controlling carefully for differences in education, class background and other relevant variables, Duncan found that about one half of the difference between black and white earnings seemed to be a direct result of racial discrimination. Similar statistical studies in Britain also imply that discrimination is a major cause of racial disparities in earnings (Heath, 1981:178–83), an interpretation supported by numerous case studies of actual work practices, as well as by the employment investigations of the Commission for Racial Equality (Smith, 1977:64–207; Braham et al., 1981).

Britain, the United States and most other industrial societies now have comprehensive legislation prohibiting racial and ethnic discrimination in employment but the problem remains, as with housing, in enforcing the law over often complex and subtle practices. The 1976 British Race Relations Act recognized the need to attack what has been termed *indirect* discrimination, measures that may not appear to be discriminatory as such and are not necessarily motivated by prejudice, but have the consequence of placing minorities at a disadvantage. The use of non-relevant selection criteria, such as formal language tests for much unskilled work; minimum height qualifications; informal recruitment methods; trade union shop floor practices, in addition to prejudiced attitudes in management and among the work force, are a formidable set of barriers standing in the path towards racial equality in the work place.

It is now some two decades since the passage of the early Civil Rights Acts of the 1960s in America and the corresponding legislation in Britain, and the limitations of these attempts to bring about equality of opportunity for minorities are starkly illustrated by the persistence of racial disadvantage. Some gains, particularly in developing a significant black middle class in America, have been achieved but the net result, as far as the black community as a whole is concerned, is disappointing. The effects of economic recession, combined with an unsympathetic political environment under the Reagan administration (Huber, 1981:2–3; Pinkney, 1984), can be seen in a variety of economic indicators. While median black family income had grown from fifty-nine per cent to sixty-two per cent of the equivalent white figure between 1960 and 1975, by 1981 it had declined again to fifty-six per cent of the white level (Reid, 1982). Towards the end of 1982, the unemployment rate for blacks was more than twice the rate for whites, and thirty per cent of black families lived beneath the Federally defined poverty level, a figure three and a half times greater than the number of whites. In terms of wealth, argu-ably a better index of economic standing than income, blacks had on average only thirty-six per cent of the value of assets owned by whites.[10]

The situation in Britain was not dissimilar, with blacks bearing a disproportionate share of the burden of recession and young West Indian males being conspicuously over-represented in the urban unemployment statistics (Cashmore & Troyna, 1982). Intense competition for a declining number of jobs hardly created conditions favourable for rectifying an historical legacy of disadvantage. It is always easier to bring about a redistribution of resources in a climate of economic expansion than during periods of stagnation and decline, where such policies provoke the bitterness of a zero-sum game. One group's gain is another's loss; and an absolute, not just a relative, decline in the living standard of the majority group is necessary to achieve greater racial equality.

If the economic consequences of the Civil Rights era have been modest – a consolidation and marginal expansion of the black middle classes rather than a radical resolution of black poverty – what of the political gains? Certainly the legal basis of political rights in the United States has been transformed. The 1965 Voting Rights Act, prohibiting literacy tests and authorizing Federal scrutiny and, if necessary, control over registration and voting, has been a landmark measure equivalent to the *Brown* decision on education. However, while the growth of black political representation and the mobilization of the black vote may be of enormous symbolic significance, a reversal of a trend that has effectively excluded blacks from the political arena since the time of Reconstruction, there is always a danger of overestimating its actual impact. In his case study of Atlanta, Stephen Burman has shown how black political leadership can all too easily end in 'an illusion of progress': 'all the advances in political representation do not seem to have altered the basic fact that the blacks' goals remain in fundamental conflict with the means available of achieving them' (Burman, 1979:451). Black political control over the inner city will always be tempered by white domination over the economic structure, radical attempts at redistribution can often be countered by an erosion of the tax base, with white-controlled businesses following the residential flight to the suburbs.

It would be wrong, however, to totally dismiss black politicians as token figures exercising the shadow, but not the substance, of power. There is evidence to suggest that most black officials are sympathetic to the policies desired and the concerns expressed by the black electorate (Karnig & Welch, 1980:108–15). Some studies have shown that in certain communities the election of black officials has resulted in major policy changes in areas that do affect the quality of life of the black community such as jobs, education and the provision of social services (Campbell & Feagin, 1975). Nevertheless, the net impact of black political mobilization has been modest: significant changes require the cooperation of at least some whites, can encounter obstruction from bureaucrats and other key decision-makers, and are rarely achieved on an inner city tax base with its disproportionate number of poor and underprivileged citizens. Furthermore, black political power has to contend not only with white economic strength, but also with the potential threat of a white political backlash.

In Britain, where there are still no black members of Parliament and few local councillors from either the West Indian or Asian communities, the politics of race relations has been as much concerned with the activities of racist groups, like the National Front in the 1970s, as with the mobilization of black voters.[11] The direct political impact of explicitly racist parties has not been great, but the indirect consequences of these neo-fascist groups and the fears of latent anti-black sentiments in the electorate indicated by the populist appeal of Enoch Powell, have been much more significant. The major political parties have adopted an essentially defensive position on race relations, reluctantly passing anti-discrimination legislation while simultaneously tightening up immigration regulations and citizenship laws in a way that affects blacks rather than whites. The existence of the National Front[12] has made the main parties more sensitive to racist opinion which has served to 'legitimize racism further, to the detriment of black British citizens, as well as to the once-true image of Britain as a tolerant, civilized society' (Taylor, 1979:145).

In an interesting comparison between racist voting in England and the USA, as indicated by support for the National Front in the former and George Wallace's vote in the urban North of the latter, Christopher Husbands has suggested that these two similar political reactions have somewhat different dynamics. In the United States, fears generated by race relations in the housing market have a more significant impact, while in Britain it is the threat of competition in employment that seems to be a more salient factor underlying support for racist political programmes (Husbands, 1979:147–74). If this is an accurate assessment, it illustrates once again how resource competition in one sphere is frequently translated into a political contest between sections of the majority and minority groups, in which a variety of strategies and tactics may be employed to maintain privileges or rectify disadvantages. It will be the net balance of power that will determine the outcome. This, in turn, will reflect the complex pattern of resource distribution and the extent of political, economic and social mobilization found among different groups.

In the final analysis, the political struggle between groups in society rests on a basis of physical force, which means that the police and the military establishment play a crucial role as an arbiter of the last resort. Relatively little academic attention has been given to the racial and ethnic composition of these two crucial institutions compared to the enormous political sensitivity of this issue. In the 1940s, Gunnar Myrdal emphasized the fact that the police were in the frontline of American race relations and that 'the Negro's most important public contact is with the policeman' (Myrdal, 1944:II,535).[13] Subsequent reports on the US riots of the 1960s and the British riots of 1981, confirm the importance of the part played by police attitudes and tactics in precipitating and escalating racial conflicts (Kerner, 1968; Scarman, 1981). The army is possibly an even more important institution in societies where the ethnic and racial balance of power is delicately poised. I have already mentioned the prominence of ethnic Russians in the officer corps of the Soviet armed forces and the ever-increasing proportion of rank and file soldiers drawn from the Central Asian republics. In the United States, the armed forces were only integrated on President Truman's orders in 1948, and there is sustained evidence of racial disparities in military justice and promotion (Hayles & Perry, 1981:44–55), as well as disproportionate casualty rates among racial minority soldiers in combat.

Although most governments deny that ethnicity or racial matters affect their military decisions, in reality it can be demonstrated that 'notions of ethnicity are vital, affecting whom to recruit and whom to exempt, whom to promote and whom to leave in the ranks, whom to channel into front-line combat units and whom to concentrate in technical jobs' (Enloe, 1980:10). Nowhere is this more true than in the Third World, and particularly plural societies, where the role of ethnic soldiers, paramilitary and police forces has been unusually prominent. In Fiji, for example, the concentration of Fijians and under-representation of Indians in the armed forces has been one major source of controversy (Norton, 1977:126). In South Africa, the military has been carefully organized to reflect racial and ethnic priorities, while in Nigeria the interaction of ethnic loyalties and military factions has been a major source of conflict in the post-independence period. As the assassination of Mrs Gandhi in 1984 by Sikh members of her personal bodyguard illustrates, the ultimate measure of racial and ethnic trust is the extent to which a society can tolerate an integrated and egalitarian army and police force.

6 The quest for racial justice

Throughout this book, I have tried to show the manner in which power relations influence the structure and dynamics of race relations. While evidence from many different societies supports this approach, it is important to stress that I am not advocating the case for total determinism. 'Men make their own history,' the young Marx claimed, 'but they do not make it as they please.' The mature Marx, and so many Marxists, seem to have abandoned this insight with their impatience for the new socialist order and their belief that they have discovered the 'science' of society. Individuals and groups do have a variety of options open to them: reactions to domination reveal a remarkable diversity in the strategies adopted to resist racial oppression or to fight attempts to suppress national consciousness. The Jews, Kurds and Armenians, to cite some conspicuous cases, have displayed enormous historical tenacity in the face of ferocious attempts to destroy their separate ethnic identity and to obliterate their very physical existence. There are, indeed, examples where the power imbalance is so overwhelming that a group is totally exterminated. The fate of the Tasmanian Aborigines is one such tragic event, and the precarious position of many tribal societies, such as the Amazonian Indians in contemporary Brazil, shows that this crime is not simply a relic of human barbarism. If men can affect their own destinies, admittedly within certain limits, then the goals and values held by individuals and groups need to be considered carefully, and the strategies they adopt to achieve such ends must be evaluated with these motives in mind.

Among most oppressed minorities the basic theme of the present century can be described as a quest for racial justice. How individuals and groups define this 'justice' is a more complex matter, but it usually includes a demand for a combination of fundamental rights: to adhere to minority religious beliefs and practices; to preserve linguistic traditions; and to exercise a measure of political self-determination. In general, this notion of justice also includes some degree of economic parity between groups, so that major differences in life styles and life chances should not occur among individuals purely on the basis of their membership of a particular group.

Underlying these racial and ethnic demands are certain conceptions of the just society, which are often implicit and not elaborated into a systematic philosophy, but which need to be examined with care. The problem is that the political philosophies of majorities are not necessarily compatible with those of minorities, which can result in a fundamental clash of wills leading to intercommunal violence and warfare. Democracy as such does not necessarily solve this dilemma – in an ironic way it may actually create it – for 'one man, one vote' can all too easily degenerate into the tyranny of the majority. Minority rights under majority rule, particularly when the minority is marked off by differences in race or ethnicity, is as much a problem today as the injustice caused by a dominant minority under colonial and similar regimes (Kirkwood, 1983:129–53).

This chapter will outline the ways in which these conflicts of interest and values are revealed in a series of fundamental dilemmas. Firstly, I will consider the changing ideologies of race relations, drawing particularly on the North American experience which has had such a great influence on worldwide patterns of race relations in the postwar era. Which of the competing arguments in answer to the question 'racially separate or together?' carries the most conviction?[1] Or is this a false dichotomy disguising the fact that some intermediate path between separatism and assimilation is the optimal strategy to secure just and harmonious group relations? There is also the special case of tribal societies in the modern world which raises the rival claims of individualism and communalism in ethnic affairs. Under what conditions is democracy compatible with ethnic and racial pluralism, or are the two inherently at loggerheads? Then there is the problem of rectifying racial injustice: is it sensible to attempt to redress past inequality by means of present inequality? Can a convincing case be made to justify the use of positive discrimination and racial quotas? The next questions to consider are the costs of intolerance and injustice in terms of the link between race, ethnicity and warfare, as well as the causes of the ultimate horror of genocide. Finally, I will attempt to summarize some major lessons that social scientists can learn from the impact of racial and ethnic diversity on society.

In North America, ideologies of race and ethnic relations have changed considerably throughout the present century. The powerful influence of the white, Anglo-Saxon Protestant (WASP) establishment made what Milton Gordon termed 'Anglo-conformity' (Gordon, 1964:87–114) a central force during the years preceding the First World War. Yet what was to be a major influence on white immigrant groups was rarely considered applicable to the racial minorities of blacks, Indians or Chinese. As the power of the WASP elite was increasingly challenged, an alternative model of group relations developed based on the analogy of the melting pot. Religious, national and, among its more enthusiastic exponents, racial groups would be melted down to form the basis of a unique American identity. The vision of a new society that would not merely assimilate, but would synthesize the cultural and social characteristics of all groups had an enormous appeal to those Poles, Irish, Italians and Jews who made up the massive migrations across the Atlantic at the turn of the century. Despite its ideological attractions, the melting pot was destined to be questioned in its turn, during the postwar period, by a new orthodoxy of ethnic pluralism, particularly by whites who argued that American society had either progressed beyond the melting pot or, perhaps, had never actually experienced it in the first place (Glazer & Moynihan, 1970).

Another challenge to the three major ideologies of assimilation, amalgamation and integration (to give the technical terms for Anglo-conformity, the melting pot and ethnic pluralism) came from the other end of the assimilationist spectrum. A countervailing rhetoric of separatism was voiced by certain prominent figures among the elites of the various racial minorities. The separatist tradition, while never appealing to more than a minority within the minorities, had deep roots in American history. Among American Indians and certain religious sects, such as the Amish,[2] there has been a genuine desire for a totally separate communal and territorial existence. In the case of blacks, separatism has taken a variety of forms: the 'back to Africa' movements of Bishop Turner, Martin Delany and Marcus Garvey; and the demands for the creation of black states espoused by the American Communist Party in the 1930s and by the Black Muslims under the leadership of Elijah Muhammad (Stone, 1976:19–30). Modern black separatism has been of a more limited variety, such as that associated with the black power movement of the 1960s. These 'separatist' demands, however, need to be carefully interpreted for they were often as much a tactical response to the challenge of genuine integration as a true reflection of a long-term racial strategy.

There is an important distinction between the separatism of the dominant group and minority separatism. It is also essential to differentiate between 'genuine' separatism, which demands complete group autonomy within an exclusive territorial base, and those forms of 'spurious' separatism, which are used simply as a rationalization for segregation – the familiar Southern doctrine of 'separate but unequal' or the Afrikaner Nationalists' policy of apartheid. Writing about the United States at the end of the 1960s, Thomas Pettigrew commented:

The two groups of separatists have sharply different sources of motivation: the blacks to withdraw, the whites to maintain white supremacy. Nor are their assumptions on a par for destructive potential. But the danger is that black and white separatism could congeal as movements . . . and help perpetuate a racially separate and racist nation. (1971:301)

The dangers of separatism, even if it is intended as a temporary device designed to overcome the effects of discrimination, should be set against the potential advantages.

Advocates of separatism claim that conventional civil rights strategies have not achieved any significant improvement in the lives of most poor blacks. This is because, they argue, the minority lacks any meaningful control over its own affairs which is the only way to bring about worthwhile change. An integrated leadership tends to be unable or unwilling to implement the substantial transfer of resources that would be the necessary precondition of a society founded on racial justice. What is required is the mobilization of the black community to end exploitation and to liberate itself from a situation which amounts to 'internal colonialism' (Blauner, 1972). The problem with this analysis is that it neglects the extent to which separatism places the burden of improvement on the black community itself, a community already disproportionately suffering from economic disadvantage and social deprivation.

Isolation can also perpetuate negative group perceptions and lead to certain individuals, both black and white, retaining a vested interest in preserving a number of protected positions and monopolies generated by the communal insulation of the racial or ethnic ghetto from the wider society. While there may be some initial advantage in terms of political consolidation, and an enhanced sense of group identity and pride, this policy can easily degenerate into a substitute for a concerted attack on all forms of discrimination. It is worth noting that separatism and integration are not mutually exclusive tactics, and that a selective form of separation combined with the vigorous pursuit of equal rights in the major institutions of society, can be a quite logical strategy to follow. The case for a total and exclusive separatism, even if it had any practical reality, is much more problematic. As one of its leading American critics points out: 'To prescribe more separation because of discomfort, racism, conflict, or the need for autonomy is like getting drunk again to cure a hangover. The nation's binge of apartheid must not be exacerbated but alleviated' (Pettigrew, 1971:327–8).

The comparison with South Africa's racial policies is particularly interesting. In that society there has been a fierce debate about the relative merits of exclusive racial organizations, as opposed to multiracial alliances, as a political means to secure the end of white minority rule. A split between the African National Congress (ANC), with its non-racial philosophy, and the Pan African Congress (PAC), led exclusively by Africans, was, in part, engendered by different interpretations of the role of whites in the liberation struggle. The Nationalists' racial policies in South Africa pose difficult problems for the opposition, for to employ separatist means to attack a doctrine which, at least in theory, argues for the separation of racial groups in society, does appear to be dangerously contradictory. Similarly, those African politicians, like Gatsha Buthelezi, who are opposed to apartheid and favour a unitary, non-racial state, but who nevertheless accept positions as leaders of the so-called 'homelands' (as the only practical means of attacking the system from within), are placed in an embarrassing dilemma.[3] No matter how much they may protest against the present regime, the fact that they are prepared to hold office in one of the 'tribal states' envisaged under the apartheid blueprint, can be interpreted as an implicit recognition of the permanent fragmentation of the country along racial and ethnic lines.

While separatism as a tactical method or as a strategic goal is fraught with ambiguity, there may be certain circumstances where it is more convincingly justified. The partition of Ireland and of India took place amid terrible bloodshed, but some would argue that without these territorial divisions the level of communal slaughter would have been even greater. A strong case for a certain measure of separatism can be made with respect to those simpler communal societies facing what Frances Svensson has aptly called 'the final crisis of tribalism' (Svensson, 1978:100–23). Under these conditions the pursuit of manifestly universalistic policies is usually disastrous and may have the same cynical latent functions as the Bantustan programme in the application of apartheid. In this respect comparisons between American and Russian policies towards their respective tribal peoples are particularly instructive. In both societies, tribal peoples comprise small minorities of barely one million individuals who have encountered the dominant groups in frontier conditions over a period of several centuries. There is an important distinction between the extent to which American Indians and Siberian tribal peoples have had to compete for resources with in-coming settlers: much of the North American Great Plains was fertile agricultural land, in contrast to the tundra and taiga which clearly could not support heavy settlement. Nevertheless, there have been interesting differences in policies and philosophies concerning the status of the tribal peoples in the wider society.

In the Russian case, under both the Tsarist and Soviet regimes, a more gradual, evolutionary strategy towards an ultimate goal of assimilation has been the predominant approach. Policies towards the American Indians, however, have followed a much more radical path, attempting to assimilate Indians into an individualistic culture and society simply by destroying the foundations of a communally based identity. The Russians searched for a compromise between uniformity and separatism, coopting native leadership into the administrative structure, yet interfering minimally in local community affairs. Under the Native Code of 1822, the Russian authorities established certain influential principles: the recognition of traditional leaders and customary law; the regulation of commerce and industry to prevent the grosser forms of exploitation between settlers and natives; and a taxation policy related to the tribal peoples' capacity to pay. This basic approach was continued after the Russian revolution so that, 'the principle of balancing separateness with uniformity was one which the Soviet regime was to continue in its tribal policies of the twentieth century, and with it, curiously enough, a strategy of evolution rather than revolution in tribal affairs' (Svensson, 1978:108).

In contrast, the policy of the United States, after the tribes' military resistance had been crushed in the early 1870s, was aimed at the rapid integration of the Indians into the mainstream of society, as if they were simply another ethnic group to be absorbed in the American melting pot. The Allotment Act of 1887 sought to break up the reservations and reallocate communal lands on the basis of individual ownership. During the following half century, Indian land holdings were reduced from 150 to 40 million acres. At the same time, native religious practices were suppressed; the use of Indian languages discouraged or forbidden; and the authority of traditional leaders undermined. The whole American democratic ethos, based as it was on 'a model of the competitive, individualistic marketplace of economic theory' (ibid, 106), challenged the fundamental values of Indian society.[4]

It is true that there were subsequent countertrends in both Soviet and United States policies, with draconian forms of forced collectivization attempted briefly under Stalin in the 1930s, and a more 'open', communally sensitive administration introduced during the same period in America. After the Second World War, however, the two policies reverted to their traditional courses. The Soviet authorities returned to a gradualism in tribal administration, while the American government favoured the 'termination' of separate status and made determined attempts to force Indians off the reserves and into urban employment. This contrast between the two different approaches in no sense reflects a greater Soviet tolerance towards all minorities (as is clear from the discussion in chapter three). Nevertheless, the Russian autocracies have been more willing to allow what Svensson has called 'policy space', a protective separatism that seeks to utilize elements of the tribal culture as a means of easing the path towards modernization, than the more radical assimilationism of American democracy.

Not all policies of separation are necessarily favourable to tribal peoples, as Colin Tatz has forcefully argued in relation to the present predicament of the Australian Aborigines (Tatz, 1980:281–302). Even legislation purporting to protect the Aborigines from white depredations can easily be used to 'incarcerate subject people in segregated institutions', so that in 'guarding Aborigines the protections became discriminations' (ibid, 285). Like all tribal peoples the Aborigines are relatively powerless in terms of numbers, technology and organization when confronted by the coercive strength of the modern state or the connections and influence of the multinational corporations. In the past, the classic response has been to retreat into inhospitable deserts or mountain areas when contacts have proved to be too threatening or attempts at resistance suicidal (Reynolds, 1982). The development of modern techniques of mineral exploration and extraction and the increasing expansion of communication networks have resulted in renewed resource competition[5] in previously remote and uncontested areas. Once again, this has exposed the powerlessness of tribal peoples to resist infringements on their few remaining rights.

Three possible reactions have been attempted: political mobilization to achieve some leverage on the dominant power structure; the use of the media and international pressure to expose the worst abuses of majority rule; and the resort to legal remedies to fight for justice by means of international,[6] constitutional and common law. However, despite some improvements in the climate of Australian race relations, progress has been slow which reflects the overwhelming imbalance of power between blacks and whites in the country. In the words of one observer:

Queensland and West Australia continue to fulminate, and to act, against Aboriginal interests and Aborigines generally. They fiddle elections, tamper with votes, brush aside religious sensitivities, bulldoze sacred ground, negate land acquisition, dismiss councils and whitewash royal commission findings of police violence and abuse of authority. (Tatz, 1980:299)

Can it be argued, then, that democracy and racial justice are only compatible under conditions where racial and ethnic groups share a balance of power? Or is it more plausible to suggest that plural societies simply do not possess the essential preconditions that allow liberal democracy to develop and survive? The answer to these questions is in fact very complicated and can perhaps be best explored in relation to the debate over what Arend Lijphart has called 'consociational democracy' (Lijphart, 1968). He has defined consociational democracy as a form of government by elite cartel designed to turn a society with a 'fragmented political culture' into a stable democracy (Lijphart, 1977:216). The distinctive feature of this system is a coalition government in which the various partners can all veto major decisions. Ethnic leaders are elected by proportional representation and there is a considerable measure of autonomy granted to each ethnic or racial sub-community to run its own internal affairs. Thus a modified form of democracy is developed in order to reconcile the potential conflict between majority rule and minority rights. By incorporating minorities into the political decision-making process, the majority gains a greater measure of stability and loyalty to the state, while the minority no longer fears permanent political exclusion because it can never command sufficient votes to challenge the governing majority's grip on power.

Critics of consociationalism maintain that it is a model based on the experience of a few, rather unusual, European societies, such as Holland, Belgium, Switzerland and Austria, and can in no sense be seen as a feasible political system for most plural societies in the contemporary world. Countries such as Cyprus, Malaysia and Lebanon, which have attempted to follow a consociational pattern of government, have not been able to sustain it for long. Alvin Rabushka and Kenneth Shepsle (1972) have developed a theory of democratic instability which, they claim, is the inevitable consequence of politics in plural societies. These societies consist of groups holding incompatible values so that when political mobilization takes place the resulting ethnic and racial parties ensure the collapse of a democratic party system. A short-term unity in the face of a common enemy, as in the last stages of colonialism, may occur but this will rapidly deteriorate once the external force is removed.

The relative size and strength of different groups can affect the particular outcome but rarely in a manner that will sustain democratic procedures. If one group represents an absolute majority, then smaller groups will be tempted to by-pass elections which they cannot hope to win and resort to other means of obtaining power, as in the case of the familiar military coups of post-colonial Africa. If groups are evenly balanced, then power is crucially affected by demographic trends such as differential birthrates or levels of migration, and the mere suggestion of a new census becomes a highly charged, if not an explosive, issue. Despite a certain plausibility, Rabushka and Shepsle's argument that ethnic parties are the fundamental cause of democratic instability is not totally convincing, and a series of other factors may well be the basis of both the party structure and the lack of democracy. The sudden creation of a mass electorate; the birth of democracy under violent circumstances; unrealistic expectations concerning the state's capacity to promote economic growth; and the existence of an established state bureaucracy prior to the introduction of universal franchise, are all important variables determining the final outcome (van Amersfoort & van der Wusten, 1981:476–85).

In response to these criticisms, Lijphart and other consociationalists claim that, under suitable conditions, a form of democracy is viable in communally divided societies. Many factors will influence the probability of this outcome: whether there is a balance of power among the various groups; the existence of a political culture favouring compromise rather than conflict, which may itself be the result of a previous history of violence; and the strategic significance of the society within the international political order. The role of outside forces in the collapse of the Lebanese consociation is one clear illustration of this last point. Some scholars have even suggested that a consociational political structure could provide a viable basis for peaceful change in South Africa (Hanf et al., 1981), which seems to be a remarkably optimistic interpretation of the available evidence. On balance, the prospects of successfully combining liberal democracy with a society which is deeply divided by racial and ethnic barriers are not good, but they may well be improved when communal divisions are not superimposed on substantial economic and social differences.

This is one major argument in favour of adopting extraordinary measures to achieve greater ethnic and racial equality. In recent years, a fundamental debate has taken place on whether racial justice demands not simply equality of opportunity, but some approximation to equality of results. Can this be, and should it be – for this is a moral question as well – attempted by an explicit policy of positive or 'reverse' discrimination? There are few issues that have proved to be more controversial than the question of the merits and drawbacks of racial quotas as a development of anti-discrimination measures. Unlike previous civil rights strategies, this dispute has divided opinion even among 'liberal' allies sharing the same ultimate goal of eliminating racism in society.

The problem may be stated as follows. By the end of the 1960s, American race relations legislation had established a framework whereby acts of discrimination motivated by overt prejudice against racial or ethnic groups were declared unambiguously illegal. However, much discrimination did not take this direct form, for many practices which had grown up during a history of racial inequality meant that, even if there was no racist intent, they would still place racial minorities at a gross disadvantage. This situation became known as *institutional* discrimination, and was recognized in legislation and in legal rulings as a fundamental obstacle in the path towards racial justice. A dilemma arises, however, when the only effective policies to meet this problem appear to involve treating individuals differently on racial grounds.

Throughout the 1970s, civil rights organizations and the courts increasingly supported more vigorous types of 'affirmative action' measures. These did not stop at the systematic encouragement of minorities to apply for places in educational institutions, training programmes and employment, but actually gave preference to minority candidates over equally, or even better, qualified white applicants. This resulted in a series of legal cases in which the litigants claimed that their constitutional rights to equal treatment under the law, guaranteed by the Fourteenth Amendment of the American Constitution, were being denied by such selection procedures. As a result of the *DeFunis*, *Bakke* and *Weber* cases, which were concerned with admissions policies to university or training programmes, the principles underlying these procedures were clarified. This led to a qualified acceptance of reverse discrimination, provided it was implemented in a flexible manner and on a temporary basis. In 1980, Justice Marshall summed up the philosophy in his Supreme Court opinion, declaring that society had a duty to promote 'meaningful equality of opportunity, not an abstract version of equality in which the effects of past discrimination would be forever frozen into our social fabric'.

One of the most cogent criticisms of this approach was argued by Nathan Glazer in his controversial book *Affirmative Discrimination* (1975).[7] Glazer maintained that the use of quotas, based on a statistical assumption that the under-representation of minorities in a particular type of employment or educational programme must necessarily be attributed to racial discrimination, was a dangerous and misguided procedure. The concept of 'institutional racism' was too crude and all- embracing, leading to the false conclusion that any attempt to make distinctions between individuals was both unjust and illegal. Even if such objections were deemed insufficient to override the net social benefit of a more egalitarian and racially just society, there were further arguments against such a strategy. Quotas rapidly become institutionalized, they are easier to introduce than to end, and yet their justification can only be sustained while racial imbalances persist. Secondly, they tend to benefit only one section of the black community, the emergent middle class, leaving the more fundamental problem of poverty in the urban ghetto largely untouched. Thirdly, they run counter to the trend of anti-discrimination policy which asserts the primacy of individual rights over group membership, thereby 'emphasizing rigid lines of division between ethnic groups and making the ethnic characteristics of individuals . . . primary for their personal fate' (Glazer, 1975:70). Finally, they will have the effect of devaluing minority qualifications in the eyes of the wider society and thereby undermine the self-esteem of the group as a whole.

The considerable gains made by blacks in America during the 1960s were achieved, according to Glazer, by the attack on direct discrimination and not by applying the principle of proportional representation. Such a policy would not solve the problem of the urban underclass, associated with the substantial growth of female-headed families, youth unemployment and crime, and was therefore an ineffective remedy for the severe deprivation of the low-income, black population of the inner city. However, the scope of quotas and preferential hiring is not limited to the black community, and the arbitrary nature of which groups to include, and which to exclude, produces further anomalies. Are all Americans with Spanish surnames, including the Cubans, and all Orientals, such as the Japanese, in greater need of compensatory assistance than individuals from other groups, such as the Acadians (French Canadians) or the white rural poor? The rough justice of this form of group categorization can easily produce a reactive response by excluded groups or elements of the dominant majority, provoking racial and ethnic conflict and polarizing society on a communal basis. The 'white ethnic' revival during the 1970s can reasonably be interpreted in these terms, as an attempt to tap the material rewards of ethnic identification, so that liberal efforts to compensate for past injustices have the unintended and ironic consequence of generating a highly illiberal political climate.

As in the argument over busing, opinions among social scientists vary about the wisdom of these measures because the net balance of costs and benefits is hard to assess. While Glazer raises important questions about the advisability of reverse discrimination, his conclusions can be attacked on a number of grounds. Firstly, his concern with individuals *qua* individuals, outside their social milieu, is a surprising perspective for a sociologist and, more particularly, for the co-author of *Beyond the Melting Pot*, with its emphasis on the way that New York's Irish, Italians and Jews have used their collective strength to gain economic and political favours. Blacks, Hispanics and American Indians have had to contend with these entrenched ethnic interests and have turned to Federal political intervention to challenge these local ethnic monopolies. As a result, the quotas demanded by these groups are 'out in the open for public scrutiny, not under the table or behind closed doors or in the cigar-smoke-filled back rooms at City Hall where police captains and fire chiefs are appointed and where local business and construction deals get made in this nation so committed to individual merit' (Duster, 1978:254). It is the visibility of the system, not its underlying principle, that is the new departure.

A second criticism of Glazer's analysis is that he exaggerates the degree of progress made by the black community during the 1960s, even among those gaining access to professional, technical and other middle-class occupations. The comparison he makes between the rates of increase in black and white employment in these categories is deceptive, for groups that start at a low base figure will inevitably appear to make high proportional gains in the early stages of any overall improvement. Whether this initial black progress can be sustained, and the fact that the absolute advantage of whites over blacks may be increasing, are more relevant considerations. Experience of the economic recession since Glazer wrote his book in the early 1970s, and particularly the disproportionate impact of unemployment on minority youth, raises further doubts about the effectiveness of a purely negative strategy towards racial discrimination.

Another type of argument has also been used to answer the critics of reverse discrimination. This is not so much focused on the practical difficulties surrounding the policies, as the moral issue of whether such discrimination is simply unjust.

To give favoured treatment to black candidates merely because they are members of a particular minority, it is claimed,
results in injustice when poor white individuals, who may
have suffered from greater disadvantages than favoured
blacks, are excluded from benefits under the quota system.
The validity of this argument depends on the type of justification used to support positive discrimination. A case based on
'compensatory justice' is obviously weakened by the fact that
the blacks who benefit are usually those who have suffered
least from past injustice, while the section of the white community that is made to shoulder the whole burden generally
comprises those who have gained the least from historical
patterns of exploitation. The only convincing *moral* argument
is, as Ronald Dworkin has rightly stressed, one that points to
the future benefit that such policies may be expected to generate for the community as a whole (Dworkin, 1977; 1981).

In other spheres of social policy, the principle of discrimi-
nating between individuals on what is essentially an arbitrary
basis (e.g. the distribution of 'intelligence') in order to achieve
wider social goals (the optimal use of social resources) is firmly
established. It is a measure of the sensitivity of race relations
that analogous proposals applied to this field provoke such
controversy.[8] I have concentrated on the American experience
to illustrate this dilemma since it has provided the most
sophisticated level of debate about the issue. In Britain, parallel arguments have been generated in the aftermath of Lord
Scarman's report on the 1981 riots, and by the need to review
the effectiveness of legal measures against discrimination several years after the passage of the 1976 Race Relations Act
(Lustgarten, 1980; McCrudden, 1983).

Ethnic quotas in other societies have also proved to be
highly controversial, if not explosive, issues. Less than a year
before the outbreak of Sinhalese-Tamil violence in Sri Lanka
during 1983, the government had decided to implement an
ethnic quota system with respect to university admissions and
employment in the public sector. A government spokesman
claimed that:

Under this system the majority community [in this case the Sinhalese who constitute almost eighty per cent of the population and who are the dominant political group] will have the assurance that opportunities in these fields to members of other communities are subject to a ceiling and that there will be no undue erosion of its legitimate share. Also the minority community will have a sense of relief that they are guaranteed their quota . . . This will go a long way to create an atmosphere of harmony among members of all communities. (Udalagama, 1982)

These measures were attacked by the Tamil minority, who for historical reasons have been relatively well educated and prosperous, as 'pandering to Sinhalese chauvinism' and they renewed their demand that 'merit' should be the sole criterion for admission to the universities and the public service.

Violence has also been associated with attempts in India to create a more egalitarian society, despite the traditional strength of the caste system, by reserving places in colleges and educational institutions for Harijans (untouchables) and tribal peoples. During February 1981, to cite just one example, at least twenty people were killed in Gujarat state in riots stimulated in part by the state government's reservation policy (Fishlock, 1981). Clearly there is no simple answer to the question of whether quotas and positive discrimination constitute a legitimate and effective strategy to achieve a greater measure of racial justice. The outcome will depend on a careful weighing of costs and benefits, and the context and circumstances under which such policies are pursued.

The degree of violence so frequently generated by racial and ethnic relations raises a further set of fundamental issues that have been subject to remarkable neglect by all but a few social scientists. Two of the most extreme manifestations of violence, warfare and genocide, are rarely even mentioned in standard textbooks on race relations, or are casually relegated to a passing footnote as if they are peripheral to the topic. Yet who would dispute the relevance of racial and ethnic divisions to the analysis of modern warfare? Who could deny that the shadow of genocide, conceived as the horrific 'final solution' to ethnic and racial diversity, hangs like a sword of Damocles over the conscience of twentieth-century man?

One extreme argument maintains that it will be a 'race war', not class conflict or a war between states, that will fuel the fires of the next major outburst of global violence. In his polemical book entitled *The Race War*, written in the middle of the 1960s, Ronald Segal presented a stark vision of a world becoming increasingly unstable because of the coincidence of colour and wealth, leading inevitably to a catastrophic showdown between the rich white and the poor non-white regions of the globe. Segal's thesis has been rightly criticized for its gross oversimplification: the obsession with racial divisions underplays equally fundamental cultural, religious and regional barriers that may often cut across 'racial' groups; he ignores the strength of many 'non-white' states, the military might of China or the economic muscle of Japan; and his naive anticipation of a successful struggle of the powerless against the powerful overlooks the obvious conclusion that such a race war would quickly degenerate into a race massacre. Race and ethnic conflict are important elements in modern warfare, but their dynamics do not operate according to a simplistic racial dialectic.

The relationship is far more complex than is suggested by any sharp polarity of black and white. A more considered evaluation of the connection between war and ethnicity in general points to an intricate form of reciprocal causality in which ethnic and racial communities not only wage wars, but are also shaped and even created by them. After a wide-ranging survey of the historical and comparative evidence, Anthony Smith has concluded that, contrary to most conventional assumptions, warfare is a major independent factor in the development of ethnic consciousness and that it has an important, though variable, impact on the cohesion of different societies (Smith, 1981a:375–97). The effects will depend on the character and the duration of the conflict: whether it is a total war, involving mass conscription and mobilization, or a much more limited exercise undertaken by a small professional army. In the former situation, the conflict is likely to have a more profound impact on the ethnic structure of the society, and the longer the duration of the hostilities, the greater the strain on the ethnic unity of the state.

Wars have often undermined multinational states, such as the Habsburg and Ottoman empires, while the Second World War played its part in the process of decolonization. The internal solidarity of Vietnam and Israel, to take two radically different societies, has probably been assisted by a generation of continuous armed conflict, while from an even longer perspective 'many European states – England, France, Russia, Switzerland, Spain, Poland and Sweden among them – have been beaten into "national shape" by the hammer of incessant wars, which have also endowed them with a great part of their ethnic cohesion and imagery' (Smith, 1981a:391).

Warfare has also been linked to that other much neglected problem of genocide.[9] Although it is true that some of the most appalling atrocities have taken place in the midst of wars, the connection between war and genocide is not a simple causal one. Some genocidal massacres have been perpetrated when there has been no serious interstate hostility; many wars have not been associated with systematic campaigns to slaughter whole communities (Kuper, 1981:11–18). But the attempt to annihilate every man, woman and child belonging to a specific religious, ethnic or racial group is not an entirely random flight into collective madness. There are certain conditions that are more likely to encourage genocidal massacres and certain societies with a higher potential for genocide than others. In the same way as I have argued in relation to other problems in the field of race relations, there is no single, simple explanation for a phenomenon of enormous complexity which, within the present century alone, has claimed as its victims peoples as diverse as Armenians and Jews, Chinese and Ibo, Hutus and Bangladeshis.

Having defined genocide as 'a special form of murder: state sanctioned liquidation against a collective group, without regard to whether an individual has committed any specific and punishable transgression', Irving Horowitz (1980:1) argues that societies should be classified according to the extent to which the state permits the official destruction of its people. This is a distinction of such importance that it should be a basic criterion in the construction of typologies of societies and, while most states have some genocidal skeletons lurking in their historical cupboards, actual 'genocidal societies' must be viewed as qualitatively different from all others. Despite the moral simplicity of this position, it does raise a series of problems, for many states that appear to be superficially alike are in reality quite different. The fascism of Nazi Germany had a far greater genocidal impact than that of Italy or Spain; while the human destructive capacity of Soviet Russia, although based on eliminating political dissent rather than motivated by racial extermination, has rivalled that of the Nazis. What then are the principal social and ideological foundations of genocide?

A few sociologists have attempted to isolate the more important factors that appear to be causally related to the incidence of genocidal destruction. One element that is of central significance is major differences in group power, a recurrent theme affecting all aspects of race and ethnic relations. Massacres perpetrated against tribal peoples are a clear example of this imbalance for, as Leo Kuper has noted, 'the ability of a group to defend itself, and to exact reprisals, is of course some guarantee against genocide' (Kuper, 1981:322). While enormous imbalances in power are crucial, other variables also play a part in determining whether genocidal potential is translated into an actual policy of physical destruction. The suitability of a group for exploitation as a slave or cheap labour force can act as one restraint on the destruction of what may be viewed as a useful asset by the dominant group. Colonial dependence on native labour has produced 'infrastructural contradictions', to use Sartre's term, which stand in the way of genocide. Terror and violence may be necessary to instil fear and secure acquiescence but systematic slaughter, unless there is a limitless supply of new victims, becomes counterproductive. Those groups that have been unable to resist colonial invasion, and have proved to be unsuitable or simply unwilling to adapt to the demands of the colonial economy, have been exceptionally vulnerable to mass extermination.

Where there has been competition for land, either for farming or the extraction of mineral resources, and when there has been no sanctuary into which a threatened group can retreat – 'inhospitable' deserts, mountains or forests, or a 'homeland' beyond the dominant group's control – then genocide becomes an increasingly probable prospect. It is usually in the early phase of colonial conquest, as well as in the final stages of the colonial era with its attendant power struggles that frequently spill over into the post-colonial period, that the genocidal response is most common. Under these conditions, imbalances of power and fierce group competition fuse together to support 'dehumanizing' ideologies which can all too easily result in a cold, calculating slaughter. Many tribal peoples have been literally hunted as animals in frontier situations, while a parallel process of bureaucratic dehumanization has been a feature common to many of the accounts of the Nazi concentration camps.

The association between genocide and plural societies is in part related to the impact of colonialism. Middleman minorities, whose presence has been closely linked to imperial policies, have proved to be frequent targets of attack (Fein, 1979:89). This is because they combine several dangerous features: they are relatively powerless in political, military and demographic terms; they occupy high-profile, competitive roles which increase economic friction and open up the prospects of lucrative plunder; and they are easily identifiable on account of racial and cultural difference which makes them ideal candidates to serve as scapegoats for ruthless and threatened elites. Although it is often claimed that genocidal massacres are 'spontaneous' eruptions of mass hostility towards historical enemies or despised 'pariah' groups, in reality most recorded acts of genocide are either committed at the behest of ruling groups or with their flagrant collusion. It is one of the tragic ironies of the modern world that technological sophistication has not solved the basic problems of human relationships, but merely enabled conflicts to be pursued with greater destructive force and hideous efficiency.

*

This analysis of genocide and war brings the discussion full circle. Social scientists have gradually recognized that the whole field of race and ethnic relations is not simply a specialist preoccupation on the side lines of the discipline, but an area that poses some of the most fundamental problems facing any analyst of societal relations and social change. The major lessons that emerge from this and previous chapters can be summarized in the following brief points.

Most patterns of race and ethnic relations have developed out of a complex mixture of causal factors. Among these factors differences in power, wherever they occur, from colonial frontier situations to the inner cities of urban-industrial societies, play a crucial part in determining the outcome of group relations. Power must be defined in its broadest sense to include class, status and political elements, as well as organizational, bureaucratic and military resources. No single variable can provide a sufficient explanation for the diversity of possible results, and an exaggerated emphasis on material or biological theories should be greeted with the utmost scepticism. Theories that claim to show an inevitable historical development are equally false. The notion of 'social progress' – that ethnocentric myth of the nineteenth century – should have died long ago, having been buried beneath the guilt of the racial history of the twentieth century. The Nazis could hardly claim to have progressed beyond the social philosophy and morality of Genghis Khan. Most trends in race relations are neither inevitable nor irreversible: man is a product of society, but equally he is instrumental in shaping its destiny. Fatalism in race relations is usually an excuse for the perpetuation of present injustice.

Policies designed to influence the course of race and ethnic relations must be assessed in their social and political context. Separatism and 'separate development' may be benign and just in some circumstances, and during certain historical periods, but can also be predatory and unjust at other times and in other places. Quotas aimed at rectifying the legacy of racial disadvantage should be distinguished from those motivated solely by a dominant group's desire to protect its privileges by excluding upwardly mobile members of minorities. The acid test of most policies is provided by the old maxim *cui bono?*: who stands to gain, and therefore who will lose, from such measures? Those planning changes in entrenched patterns of race and ethnic relations must consider the responses of all groups affected by their actions, weigh the costs and the benefits of these strategies, and adopt a realistic time scale before reaching a verdict on the success or failure of such schemes. It is most improbable that any political regime can reverse the consequences of centuries of discrimination in the course of a single decade. In the field of race and ethnic relations, as in most areas of social life, there are few simple problems, and still fewer simple solutions. Looking to the future, there is only one prediction that can be made with little fear of contradiction: there will be no racial peace without racial justice.

Notes

1 Race relations without races?

1. This was not a perfect correlation – the Zulus destroyed a substantial part of the British army in South Africa at Isandhlwana in 1879 and the Japanese inflicted a humiliating defeat on the Russians in 1905 – but these were the exceptions that proved the rule.

2. The basic distinction between racial and ethnic groups depends on whether the defining characteristics are believed to be biological or are based on religious, linguistic or other cultural variables. In practice, the question of terminology is complex and subject to considerable debate which has more than just semantic significance. See the usage employed in Stephan Thernstrom (1980) and the pertinent comments by M. G. Smith (1982). Also E. E. Cashmore (1985).

3. An early observer of the Black Muslims dismissed their political strength in the following terms: 'The stark reality is that there can be no substantial or disruptive political action by the Nation of Islam other than that akin to the campus gadfly – a nuisance, mildly frightening, but actually not as deadly as the tse-tse fly' (Essien-Udom, 1966:275).

4. One of the rare cases of consolidation after decolonization occurred with the merging of the former British and French colonies of the Cameroons to form the Federal Republic of Cameroun (Kirkwood, 1965:123).

5. See the distinction made by Andreski between the more 'rational' anti-Semitism of Eastern Europe and the psychopathological variety associated with Nazism (Andreski, 1977:125).

6. This is beautifully illustrated by the Swedish political scientist Herbert Tingsten in an article, translated by Michael Banton, on 'National Self-Examination' (Tingsten, 1979:38–54).

7. See David Lockwood's argument in 'Race, Conflict and Plural Society' (1970:57–72).

8. For a more sympathetic assessment of Park's position: Barbara Ballis Lal (1983:154–73).

9. There are numerous difficulties when trying to measure these attributes. See John J. Ray and Adrian Furnham (1984:406–12). Adorno's work has been assessed recently by Martin Jay (1984).

10. A neat illustration of this problem can be seen in the use made of Hans Eysenck's writings, despite the author's protests, by extreme right-wing politicians. See the illuminating correspondence in *The Times*, 20 March 1978.

11. The title is an echo of a famous Presidential address given by George Homans to the American Sociological Association and published as 'Bringing Men Back In' (Homans, 1964:809–18).

12. Van den Berghe's analysis of this subject is interesting, particularly when he discusses the history of Reconstruction: 'Suddenly, whites discovered a concern for the purity of their blood and rent asunder what was being forged together. They created a system of racial segregation that confined all those tainted with the stigma of African blood to pariah status, *including in many cases their own relatives*' (1981:135). (The emphasis is mine, not van den Berghe's.) The sociobiological explanation for this kin rejection remains obscure. Heribert Adam raises a related point over the position of the Cape Coloureds in South Africa (Adam, 1982:151).

2 Minority groups and power

1. See Horowitz's discussion in his paper on 'Three Dimensions of Ethnic Politics' (1971:244) and his further strictures against 'the dogma that color makes black-white differences unique in their ability to generate conflict or to produce reliable identifications of every group member. This dogma, which has no firm basis in comparative evidence, I have called the figment of pigment' (Connor, 1985).

2. There is also a high correlation between various ethnic and cultural attributes as illustrated, for example, in the perennial debate about 'Who is a Jew?'. For a recent discussion of this age-old question in relation to America see Steven M. Cohen (1983).

3. In 1951 the official figure for the total Coloured population was 1,103,000; by 1984 the estimated number was some 2,700,000 representing around 9.4 per cent of the total South African population.

4. For a clear introductory discussion of the pattern variables: Mennell (1980:40–1).

5. See the educational and family backgrounds of prominent black American leaders from Dr W. E. B. Du Bois to Dr Martin Luther King (Broderick, 1959; Franklin & Meier, 1982). The leadership among France's regionalist and nationalist groups has also been disproportionately recruited from poorly paid members of the provincial intelligentsia, particularly teachers (Beer, 1977:150).

6. Elkins's thesis that the slaves actually internalized a sense of inferiority as a result of the 'total institution' environment of the plantation, akin to that of the Nazi concentration camp, is implausible. The 'sambo stereotype' owes its origins to role-playing for survival rather than to any dramatic personality change induced by the peculiar institution (Elkins, 1959:81–139).

7. For a standard interpretation of the racial scene in Hawaii: Andrew W. Lind (1969).

8. Lieberson's later book, *A Piece of the Pie* (1980), is specifically devoted to this issue and makes a systematic attempt to compare and contrast the situation of blacks and white immigrants in the United States since 1880.

9. See the argument made by Schmitter in relation to the *Gastarbeiter* position in West Germany (1983:308–19).

10. Banton has developed this approach as a general perspective (1977b; 1983) as well as in relation to specific problem areas such as housing (1979).

3 Race relations and class

1. Fanon states his position on these issues in his major work, *The Wretched of the Earth* (1965a), and in the collections of essays entitled *A Dying Colonialism* and *Toward the African Revolution*. A general assessment of his contribution can be found in Caute (1970).

2. This shift in emphasis, which can be seen in *An Essay on Liberation* (1969) and *Counterrevolution and Revolt* (1972), makes a sharp contrast to the revolutionary 'pessimism' expressed in his most famous study, *One Dimensional Man* (1964).

3. The definitive work on this subject is undoubtedly Walker Connor's *The National Question in Marxist-Leninist Theory and Strategy* (1984).

4. For a provocative summary of the 'liberal' versus 'radical' analysis of South African history see Wright (1977), and for further thoughts on this theme, Rex (1979:246–7). Heribert Adam's recent analysis is also relevant (1984:269–82).

5. Afrikaner Nationalists and Marxists have shared at least one idea in common and that is a profound distrust for capitalists – the former because, until recently, they were drawn predominantly from the English-speaking white group; the latter because they were perceived as class enemies. It was a pact between organized (white) labour and the Nationalists that first allowed Hertzog to become prime minister in 1924, an alliance forged against Smuts who was seen as the representative of mining and business interests. See Hancock (1968).

6. Lenin also considers the consequences of this type of division in his essay on 'Imperialism and the Split in the Socialist Movement' (1942:337–51).

7. Miles continues this argument in his later paper on 'Marxism versus the Sociology of Race Relations' (1984:217–37).

8. For a fascinating account of the life of a black communist in the South during the 1930s, see Nell Irvin Painter, *The Narrative of Hosea Hudson* (1979); and for some of the reasons explaining why blacks left the party at that time: ibid (19–21).

9. I have discussed the use of these models in a comparative context in Stone (1979:255–9; 1985).

10. As Anthony Smith observes: 'Tito, Mao, Castro, Che Guevara, Ho Chi Minh, Ben Bella, Cabral, Neto, Machel are among the many socialist and communist nationalists who have been compelled by force of circumstances to modify an urban theory and wage guerrilla "peasant wars" to mobilize the countryside against the urban centres controlled by the exploiting classes' (1983:110). See also Henry Bienen's essay in Rothchild & Olorunsola (1982).

4 Race relations and social change

1. 'Modernization' implies different things to different people, but in most cases the term 'social change' is a more accurate description since it is free from evolutionary biases. These ethnocentric distortions have their origins in the social theories of the nineteenth century but their legacy has persisted into more recent times. See, for example, J. D. Y. Peel's useful critique in 'Spencer and the Neo-Evolutionists' (1969:173–91).

2. The classic study on this subject, *Industrialism and Industrial Man*, was written by Clark Kerr and his colleagues in 1960. For a reappraisal of this controversial thesis some twenty-four years later, see Clark Kerr, *The Future of Industrial Societies: Convergence or Continuing Diversity?* (1984).

3. For further clarification of the meaning of basic terms, such as state, nation, ethnic group etc., used in the literature on nationalism and ethnicity, see Walker Connor (1978:377–97).

4. There are certain cases, however, that do not fit neatly into this pattern. See, for example, the Seychelles where the superimposition of class on racial divisions has not resulted in overt ethnic or racial conflict (Low-Hang, 1984).

5. Subsequent evidence on the employment position of Ugandan Asians in Britain, Canada and India can be found in Adams & Jesudason (1984:464–79).

6. However, the developing pattern of intermarriage among the Hispanic group is interesting, see Connor (1985). For a general assessment of the position of blacks, American Indians and Hispanics see the articles by Farley, Jarvenpa and Nelson & Tienda in Alba (1985b).

7. For a more detailed analysis of the African cases, see Crawford Young (1976; 1982).

8. This is a point stressed by Cynthia Enloe in her assessment of the strategies adopted by central governments in their attempts to control separatist movements (1976:79–84).

5 Race relations and social institutions

1. For a full and up-to-date discussion of comparative slave systems, see Orlando Patterson's *Slavery and Social Death* (1984).

2. This pattern poses a further problem for Pierre van den Berghe's ingenious, but ultimately implausible, sociobiological explanation of sexual relations under slavery – the anomalous position of the white woman and her genetic inheritance. Obviously genes are not simply 'selfish' but 'sexist' too!

3. A similar result was also found in a nationwide study of American college graduates during the 1960s (Heer, 1980:517).

4. It is no coincidence that Verwoerd's early training was in psychology and sociology and that he held chairs in these subjects at Stellenbosch University before turning to a full-time political career (Hepple, 1967:16–25).

5. Ideas on these issues are subject to rapid fluctuations at least in part as a result of the general political climate. For an analysis of bilingual education under the Reagan administration, see Gaynor Cohen (1984:232–5).

6. The special character of the modern South as a region has been discussed by John Shelton Reed (1980:40–51; 1982).

7. There is a vast, and constantly growing, literature on multicultural education in Britain. For a useful recent collection of articles, see Craft (1984).

8. For an analysis of the determinants of bilingualism in Wales: McAllister and Mughan (1984:321–41).

9. The third and latest of the influential PEP (now PSI) surveys of racial disadvantage in Britain revealed that the earlier patterns of racial inequality found in the 1967 and 1974 surveys had not changed significantly (Brown, 1984).

10. The general evidence from social and economic indicators appears to endorse this picture. According to a leading financial journal: 'Data from the 1980 census and later surveys by the [census] bureau show that since the early 1970s, blacks have experienced economic setbacks influenced by growing unemployment, increases in divorce and separation rates and a rise in the number of households headed by women . . . recession and inflation through 1982 eroded black family income and contributed to an increase in poverty among blacks, especially women. The economic setbacks tended to overshadow substantial improvements over the past decade in blacks' educational attainment, school enrollment and home ownership . . .' (*Wall Street Journal*, 22.8.1983); see also the *New York Times*, 28.8.1983. See also Farley (1985).

11. For more details concerning the recent politics of race in Britain: Layton-Henry (1984:145–78); and on the activities of the National Front: Fielding (1981); Husbands (1983).

12. The same reaction is also true in France with the success of Jean-Marie Le Pen's *Front National* in the elections during 1983 and 1984.

13. Abner Cohen remarks in relation to London's Notting Hill carnival: 'Some West Indians have even argued that the police should appear in a band in the carnival procession, as is the case in Trinidad. At the same time, the police represent to many black people, particularly to the youth, evil, oppression and violence. Indeed, one carnivalist remarked once that masquerading bands do not need to represent the traditional devil – the police are there!' (1982:38). The relationship between the police and black youth has also been stressed in Scarman's report on the 1981 riots in Brixton (Scarman, 1981; Benyon, 1984).

6 The quest for racial justice

1. This question was originally posed by Thomas Pettigrew in a Presidential address to the American Psychological Association in 1968 (Pettigrew, 1971 in 1977:375–99).

2. The classic study of the Amish is by John A. Hostetler (3rd edn 1980).

3. For a critical analysis of P. W. Botha's constitutional changes which can be interpreted as an attempt to coopt the Coloured and Indian communities, but which totally exclude the African majority in South Africa: du Toit & Theron (1986).

4. The fundamental conflict between social theories based on individualistic, as opposed to communal, premises is discussed in relation to Canada's Indian population by Boldt & Long (1984:480–95).

5. In his study of Australian attitudes towards Aborigines, Ray makes the following interesting comments on this issue: 'The failure of working class people to be prejudiced against Aborigines in New South Wales reflects the fact that Aborigines are not to them an economic threat. Since Aborigines are few in absolute numbers and are very largely unemployed, they do not provide the economic competition that minorities do elsewhere. The present results certainly do make very suspect any view that the workers are intrinsically or inevitably prejudiced in their attitudes' (1981:350).

6. Thornberry (1980:249–63) provides a good summary of minority rights under international law.

7. For further essays on this theme: Glazer (1983:159–229).

8. The important distinction between 'equality of treatment' and 'treatment as equals' is often lost in the political heat generated by such moves. See Dworkin (1977; 1981); McCrudden (1983:55–74).

9. Moskos outlines several possible explanations to account for the neglect shown by sociologists, both of the right and the left, for such a fundamental issue as genocide (1980:494–5).

Bibliography

Abraham, Collin E.R. (1983), 'Racial and Ethnic Manipulation in Colonial Malaya'. *Ethnic and Racial Studies*, 6,1: 18-22.

Adam, Heribert (1979), 'Ethnic Mobilization and the Politics of Patronage in South Africa'. *Ethnic and Racial Studies*, 2,2: 139-50.

Adam, Heribert (1982), 'The Manipulation of Ethnicity: South Africa in Comparative Perspective'. In Donald Rothchild and Victor Olorunsola, eds, *State Versus Ethnic Claims*, 127-51.

Adam, Heribert (1984), 'Racist Capitalism Versus Capitalist Non-Racialism in South Africa'. *Ethnic and Racial Studies*, 7,2: 269-82.

Adam, Heribert and Hermann Giliomee (1979), *Ethnic Power Mobilized: Can South Africa Change?*. New Haven: Yale University Press.

Adams, Bert N. and Victor Jesudason (1984), 'The Employment of Ugandan Asian Refugees in Britain, Canada and India'. *Ethnic and Racial Studies*, 7,4: 464-79.

Adorno, Theodor W., Else Frenkel-Brunswick, Daniel J. Levinson and R. Nevitt Sanford (1950), *The Authoritarian Personality*. New York: Harper and Row.

Alba, Richard D. (1976), 'Social Assimilation of American Catholic National-Origin Groups'. *American Sociological Review*, 41: 1030-46.

Alba, Richard D. (1985a), 'The Twilight of Ethnicity among Americans of European Ancestry: the Case of Italians'. *Ethnic and Racial Studies*, 8,1: 134-58.

Alba, Richard D., ed. (1985b), 'Ethnicity and Race in the USA: Towards the Twenty-First Century'. Special Issue, *Ethnic and Racial Studies*, 8,1: 1-180.

Andreski, Stanislav (1977), 'An Economic Interpretation of Anti-Semitism'. In John Stone, ed., *Race, Ethnicity and Social Change*, 123-34.

Apter, David E. (1965), *The Politics of Modernization*. Chicago: Chicago University Press.

Avineri, Shlomo (1968), *Karl Marx on Colonialism and Modernization*. New York: Doubleday.

Azrael, Jeremy R., ed. (1978), *Soviet Nationality Policies and Practices*. New York: Praeger.

Baker, Donald G. (1978), 'Race and Power: Comparative Approaches to the Analysis of Race Relations'. *Ethnic and Racial Studies*, 1,3: 316-35.

Baker, Donald G. (1983), *Race, Ethnicity and Power: A Comparative Study*. London: Routledge and Kegan Paul.

Baker, Keith A. and Adriana A. de Kanter (1983), *Bilingual Education: a Reappraisal of Federal Policy*. Lexington, Mass: D.C. Heath.

Ball, H.V., G.E. Simpson and K. Ikeda (1962), 'Law and Social Change: Sumner Reconsidered'. *American Journal of Sociology*, 68: 532-40.

Banton, Michael (1977a), *The Idea of Race*. London: Tavistock.

Banton, Michael (1977b), 'Rational Choice: A Theory of Racial and Ethnic Relations'. SSRC Research Unit on Ethnic Relations, Working Paper No. 8.

Banton, Michael (1979), 'Two Theories of Racial Discrimination in Housing'. *Ethnic and Racial Studies*, 2,4: 416-27.

Banton, Michael (1983), *Racial and Ethnic Competition*. Cambridge: Cambridge University Press.

Barrera, Mario (1979), *Race and Class in the South West: A Theory of Racial Inequality*. Notre Dame, Indiana: Indiana University Press.

Barritt, Denis P. and Charles F. Carter (1972), *The Northern Ireland Problem: A Study in Group Relations*. London: Oxford University Press.

Barth, Fredrik, ed. (1969), *Ethnic Groups and Boundaries: The Social Organization of Cultural Differences*. Boston: Little, Brown.

Beer, William R. (1977), 'The Social Class of Ethnic Activists in Contemporary France'. In Milton Esman, ed., *Ethnic Conflict in the Western World*, 143-58.

Beer, William R. (1979), 'Internal Colonialism and Rising Expectations: Ethnic Activism in Contemporary France'. In Raymond L. Hall, ed., *Ethnic Autonomy – Comparative Dynamics*, 201-33.

Bell, Daniel (1960), *The End of Ideology*. Glencoe, Illinois: Free Press.

Benyon, John, ed. (1984), *Scarman and After: Essays Reflecting on Lord Scarman's Report, the Riots and their Aftermath*. Oxford: Pergamon Press.

Berreman, Gerald (1960), 'Caste in India and the United States'. *American Journal of Sociology*, 66: 120-7.

Biddiss, Michael (1970), *Father of Racist Ideology: The Social and Political Thought of Count Gobineau*. London: Weidenfeld and Nicolson.

Bienen, Henry (1982), 'The State and Ethnicity: Integrative Formulas in Africa'. In Donald Rothchild and Victor Olorunsola, eds, *State Versus Ethnic Claims*, 100-26.

Blalock, Hubert M. (1960), 'A Power Analysis of Racial Discrimination'. *Social Forces*, 39: 53-9.

Blalock, Hubert M. (1967), *Towards a Theory of Minority Group Relations*. New York: John Wiley.

Blalock, Hubert M. (1979), *Black-White Relations in the 1980s: Toward a Long-Term Policy*. New York: Praeger.

Blalock, Hubert M. (1982), *Race and Ethnic Relations*. Englewood Cliffs, New Jersey: Prentice-Hall.

Blauner, Robert (1972), *Racial Oppression in America*. New York: Harper and Row.

Blauner, Robert (1973), 'Marxist Theory, Nationality and Colonialism'. Unpublished mss.

Blumer, Herbert (1965), 'Industrialisation and Race Relations'. In Guy Hunter, ed., *Industrialisation and Race Relations: A Symposium*, 220-53. London: Oxford University Press. (Also reprinted in John Stone, ed. (1977), *Race, Ethnicity and Social Change*, 150-66.)

Bogardus, Emory S. (1928), *Immigration and Race Attitudes*. Boston: D.C. Heath.

Bogardus, Emory S. (1958), 'Racial Distance Changes in the United States During the Past Thirty Years'. *Sociology and Social Research*, 52: 127-35.

Boldt, Menno and Anthony J. Long (1984), 'Tribal Philosophies and the Canadian Charter of Rights and Freedoms'. *Ethnic and Racial Studies*, 7,4: 480-95.

Bonacich, Edna (1972), 'A Theory of Ethnic Antagonism: The Split Labor Market'. *American Sociological Review*, 37: 549-59.

Bonacich, Edna (1973), 'A Theory of Middleman Minorities'. *American Sociological Review*, 38: 583-94.

Bonacich, Edna (1974), 'Reply to Comment by Stryker'. *American Sociological Review*, 39,2: 281.

Bonacich, Edna and John Modell (1980), *The Economic Basis of Ethnic Solidarity: Small Business in the Japanese American Community*. Berkeley: University of California Press.

Braham, Peter, Ed Rhodes and Michael Pearn, eds (1981), *Discrimination and Disadvantage in Employment: The Experience of Black Workers*. London: Harper and Row/Open University Press.

Broderick, Francis L. (1959), *W.E.B. Du Bois: Negro Leader in a Time of Crisis*. Stanford: Stanford University Press.

Brown, Colin (1984), *Black and White in Britain: The Third PSI Survey*. London: Heinemann.

Bullivant, Brian M. (1981), *The Pluralist Dilemma in Education*. London: George Allen and Unwin.

Bullivant, Brian M. (1982), 'Power and Control in the Multi-Ethnic School: Towards a Conceptual Model'. *Ethnic and Racial Studies*, 5,1: 53-70.

Bulmer, Martin (1981), 'Charles S. Johnson, Robert E. Park and the Research Methods of the Chicago Commission on Race Relations, 1919-22: An Early Experiment in Applied Social Research'. *Ethnic and Racial Studies*, 4,3: 289-306.

Burgess, Elaine (1978), 'The Resurgence of Ethnicity: Myth or Reality?'. *Ethnic and Racial Studies*, 1,3: 265-85.

Burman, Stephen (1979), 'The Illusion of Progress: Race and Politics in Atlanta, Georgia'. *Ethnic and Racial Studies*, 2,4: 441-54.

Calm, Eric and Vladimir C. Fišera, eds (1980), *Socialism and Nationalism*. Nottingham: Spokesman.

Campbell, David and Joe R. Feagin (1975), 'Black Politics in the South: a descriptive analysis'. *Journal of Politics*, 37: 129-59.

Carey, A.T. (1956), *Colonial Students: A Study of the Social Adaptation of Colonial Students in London*. London: Secker and Warburg.

Carrère d'Encausse, Hélène (1980), 'The Bolsheviks and the National Question (1903-1929)'. In Eric Calm and Vladimir C. Fišera, eds, *Socialism and Nationalism*, 113-26.

Carrington, Bruce (1981), 'Schooling an Underclass: The Implications of Ethnic Differences in Attainment'. *Durham and Newcastle Research Review*, 9,47: 293-305.

Cashmore, Ernest E. (1985), *Dictionary of Race and Ethnic Relations*. London: Routledge and Kegan Paul.

Cashmore, Ernest E. and Barry Troyna, eds (1982), *Black Youth in Crisis*. London: Allen and Unwin.

Castles, Stephen and Godula Kosack (1973), *Immigrant Workers and Class Structure in Western Europe*. London: Oxford University Press.

Caute, David (1970), *Fanon*. London: Fontana.

Chan, Anthony B. (1982), 'Chinese Bachelor Workers in Nineteenth Century Canada'. *Ethnic and Racial Studies*, 5,4: 513-34.

Cleave, Peter (1979), 'The Languages and Political Interests of Maori and Pakeha Communities in New Zealand during the Nineteenth Century'. Unpublished D.Phil, University of Oxford.

Cohen, Abner (1982), 'A Polyethnic London Carnival as a Contested Cultural Performance'. *Ethnic and Racial Studies*, 5,1: 23-41.

Cohen, Gaynor (1982), 'Alliance and Conflict Among Mexican-Americans'. *Ethnic and Racial Studies*, 5,2: 175-95.

Cohen, Gaynor (1984), 'The Politics of Bilingual Education'. *Oxford Review of Education*, 10,2: 225-41.

Cohen, Steven M. (1983), *American Modernity and Jewish Identity*. London: Tavistock.

Cohen, William B. (1980), *The French Encounter with Africans: White Responses to Blacks, 1530-1880*. Bloomington and London: Indiana University Press.

Coleman, James S. (1976), 'Response to Professors Pettigrew and Green'. *Harvard Educational Review*, 46: 217-24.

Coleman, James S. (1981), 'The Role of Incentives in School Desegregation'. In Adam Yarmolinsky et al., eds, *Race and Schooling in the City*, 182-93.

Coleman, James S. et al. (1966), *Equality of Educational Opportunity*. Washington DC: US Department of Health, Education and Welfare, Office of Education.

Connor, Walker (1972), 'Nation-building or Nation-destroying?'. *World Politics*, 24: 319-55. (Also reprinted in John Stone, ed. (1977), *Race, Ethnicity and Social Change*, 238-69.)

Connor, Walker (1977), 'Ethnonationalism in the First World: The Present in Historical Perspective'. In Milton Esman, ed., *Ethnic Conflict in the Western World*, 19-45.

Connor, Walker (1978), 'A Nation is a Nation, is a State, is an Ethnic Group, is a . . . '. *Ethnic and Racial Studies*, 1,4: 377-400.

Connor, Walker (1980), 'Ethnicity, Race and Class in the United States'. *Ethnic and Racial Studies*, 3,3: 355-9.

Connor, Walker (1984), *The National Question in Marxist-Leninist Theory and Strategy*. Princeton: Princeton University Press.

Connor, Walker, ed. (1985), *Mexican-Americans in Comparative Perspective*. Washington DC: The Urban Institute Press.

Cox, Oliver C. (1948), *Caste, Class and Race: A Study in Social Dynamics*. New York: Doubleday.

Craft, Maurice, ed. (1984), *Education and Cultural Pluralism*. London: The Falmer Press.

Cross, Malcolm (1971), 'On Conflict, Race Relations, and the Theory of the Plural Society'. *Race*, 4: 478-94.

Cross, Malcolm (1978), 'Colonialism and Ethnicity: A Theory and Comparative Case Study'. *Ethnic and Racial Studies*, 1,1: 37-59.

Curson, Sheila and Peter Curson (1982), 'The Japanese in Sydney'. *Ethnic and Racial Studies*, 5,4: 478-512.

Dahrendorf, Ralf (1959), *Class and Class Conflict in Industrial Society*. London: Routledge and Kegan Paul.

Daniel, W.W. (1968), *Racial Discrimination in England*. Harmondsworth: Penguin Books.

Davis, Kingsley (1941), 'Intermarriage in Caste Society'. *American Anthropologist*, 43: 376-95.

de Vos, George and Hiroshi Wagatsuma (1966), *Japan's Invisible Race*. Berkeley: University of California Press.

Deutsch, Karl (1953), *Nationalism and Social Communication: An Inquiry into the Foundations of Nationality*. Cambridge, Mass: Harvard University Press.

Dickie-Clark, Hamish F. (1966), *The Marginal Situation: A Sociological Study of a Coloured Group*. London: Routledge and Kegan Paul.

Dignan, Don (1981), 'Europe's Melting Pot: A Century of Large-Scale Immigration into France'. *Ethnic and Racial Studies*, 4,2: 137-52.

Dollard, John (1937), *Caste and Class in a Southern Town*. New York: Harper and Row.

Dow, Leslie M. (1982), 'Ethnic Policy and *Indigenismo* in Guatemala'. *Ethnic and Racial Studies*, 5,2: 140-55.

Doyle, Bertram (1937), *The Etiquette of Race Relations in the South*. Chicago: Chicago University Press.

Dreyer, June T. (1976), *China's Forty Millions: Minority Nationalities and National Integration in the Peoples' Republic of China*. Cambridge, Mass: Harvard University Press.

du Toit, Pierre and François Theron (1986), 'The 1983 Constitution of South Africa: A Framework for Ethnic Conflict Resolution?'. *Ethnic and Racial Studies*, 9 (forthcoming).

Dumont, Louis (1970), *Homo Hierarchicus: The Caste System and its Implications*. London: Weidenfeld and Nicolson.

Duncan, Otis D. (1968), 'Inheritance of Poverty or Inheritance of Race?'. In Daniel P. Moynihan, ed., *On Understanding Poverty: Perspectives from the Social Sciences*. New York: Basic Books.

Durkheim, Emile (1964a), *The Rules of Sociological Method*. New York: Free Press.

Durkheim, Emile (1964b), *The Division of Labor in Society*. New York: Free Press.

Duster, Troy (1978), 'Review of Nathan Glazer's *Affirmative Discrimination*'. *American Journal of Sociology*, 84,1: 252-6.

Dworkin, Ronald (1977), *Taking Rights Seriously*. London: Duckworth.

Dworkin, Ronald (1981), 'Reverse Discrimination'. In Peter Braham et al., eds, *Discrimination and Disadvantage in Employment*, 333-40.

Eckberg, Douglas L. (1979), *Intelligence and Race: The Origins and Dimensions of the IQ Controversy*. New York: Praeger.

Elkins, Stanley (1959), *Slavery: A Problem in American Institutional and Intellectual Life*. Chicago: Chicago University Press.

Enloe, Cynthia (1976), 'Central Governments' Strategies for Coping with Separatist Movements'. In W.H. Morris-Jones, ed., *The Politics of Separatism*, 79-84. Institute of Commonwealth Studies, Collected Seminar Papers, No.19.

Enloe, Cynthia (1980), *Ethnic Soldiers: State Security in a Divided Society*. Harmondsworth: Penguin Books.

Epstein, Noel (1977), *Language, Ethnicity and the Schools: Policy Alternatives for Bilingual Education*. Washington DC: Washington University Institute for Educational Leadership.

Esman, Milton, ed. (1977), *Ethnic Conflict in the Western World*. Ithaca and London: Cornell University Press.

Essien-Udom, E.U. (1966), *Black Nationalism: A Search for Identity in America*. Harmondsworth: Penguin Books.

Fanon, Frantz (1965a), *The Wretched of the Earth*. London: Macgibbon and Kee.

Fanon, Frantz (1965b), *Studies in a Dying Colonialism*. New York: Monthly Review Press.

Fanon, Frantz (1967), *Toward the African Revolution*. New York: Monthly Review Press.

Farley, Reynolds (1977), 'Trends in Racial Inequalities: have the gains of the 1960s disappeared in the 1970s?'. *American Sociological Review*, 42: 189-207.

Farley, Reynolds (1985), 'Three Steps Forward and Two Back? Recent Changes in the Social and Economic Status of Blacks'. *Ethnic and Racial Studies*, 8,1: 4-28.

Fein, Helen (1979), *Accounting for Genocide: National Response and Jewish Victimization During the Holocaust*. New York: Free Press.

Fenton, Steve (1982), 'Multi-Something Education'. *New Community*, 10,1: 57-63.

Fielding, Nigel (1981), 'Ideology, Democracy and the National Front'. *Ethnic and Racial Studies*, 4,1: 56-74.

Finer, Samuel E., ed. (1966), *Vilfredo Pareto: Sociological Writings*. London: Pall Mall Press.

Fishlock, Trevor (1981), 'Police Kill Four as Mobs Go on Riot in Gujarat'. *The Times*, 23.2.81.

Foot, Paul (1965), *Immigration and Race in British Politics*. Harmondsworth: Penguin Books.

Franklin, John H. and August Meier (1982), *Black Leaders of the Twentieth Century*. Urbana: University of Illinois Press.

Frazier, E. Franklin (1947), 'Sociological Theory and Race Relations'. *American Sociological Review*, 12,3: 265-71.

Furnivall, John S. (1948), *Colonial Policy and Practice: A Comparative Study of Burma and Netherlands India*. Cambridge: Cambridge University Press.

Gans, Herbert J. (1968), 'The Ghetto Rebellions and Urban Class Conflict'. *Proceedings of the Academy of Political Science*, 29,1: 42-51. (Also reprinted in John Stone, ed. (1977), *Race, Ethnicity and Social Change*, 197-204.)

Gans, Herbert J. (1979), 'Symbolic Ethnicity: The Future of Ethnic Groups and Cultures in America'. *Ethnic and Racial Studies*, 2,1: 1-20.

Geertz, Clifford, ed. (1963), *Old Societies and New States*. New York: Free Press.

Genovese, Eugene D. (1968), *In Black and Red: Marxian Explorations in Southern and Afro-American History*. New York: Random House.

Genovese, Eugene D. (1971), 'Materialism and Idealism in the History of Negro Slavery in the Americas'. *Journal of Social History*, 4,4: 333-56.

Giddens, Anthony (1970), 'Marx, Weber and the Development of Capitalism'. *Sociology*, 4,3: 289-310.

Giddens, Anthony (1971), *Capitalism and Modern Social Theory: An Analysis of the Writings of Marx, Durkheim and Max Weber*. Cambridge: Cambridge University Press.

Glazer, Nathan (1975), *Affirmative Discimination: Ethnic Inequality and Public Policy*. New York: Basic Books.

Glazer, Nathan (1983), *Ethnic Dilemmas 1964-1982*. Cambridge, Mass: Harvard University Press.

Glazer, Nathan and Daniel P. Moynihan (1970), *Beyond the Melting Pot: the Negroes, Puerto Ricans, Jews, Italians and Irish of New York City*. (second edition) Cambridge, Mass: The MIT Press and Harvard University Press.

Glazer, Nathan and Daniel P. Moynihan, eds (1975), *Ethnicity: Theory and Experience*. Cambridge, Mass: Harvard University Press.

Glazer, Nathan and Ken Young, eds (1983), *Ethnic Pluralism and Public Policy: Achieving Equality in the United States and Britain*. London: Heinemann.

Goldhagen, Erich (1977), 'Communism and Anti-Semitism'. In John Stone, ed., *Race, Ethnicity and Social Change*, 273-85.

Goldthorpe, John (1964), 'Social Stratification in Industrial Society'. In Paul Halmos, ed., *The Development of Industrial Society*. Sociological Review Monograph No.8.

Goldthorpe, John, David Lockwood, Frank Bechofer and Jennifer Platt (1969), *The Affluent Worker in the Class Structure*. Cambridge: Cambridge University Press.

Gordon, Milton M. (1964), *Assimilation in American Life: The Role of Race, Religion and National Origins*. New York: Oxford University Press.

Goren, Arthur A. (1980), 'Jews'. In Stephan Thernstrom, ed., *Harvard Encyclopedia of American Ethnic Groups*, 571-98.

Greeley, Andrew M. (1974), *Ethnicity in the United States*. New York: John Wiley.

Greeley, Andrew M. and Christian W. Jacobsen (1978), 'Editorial Research Note'. *Ethnicity* 5,1: 1-13.

Hall, Raymond L., ed. (1979), *Ethnic Autonomy – Comparative Dynamics: The Americas, Europe and the Developing World*. Oxford: Pergamon Press.

Hancock, W. Keith (1968), *Smuts: The Fields of Force*. Cambridge: Cambridge University Press.

Hanf, Theodor, Heribert Weiland and Gerda Vierdag (1981), *South Africa: The Prospects of Peaceful Change*. Bloomington: Indiana University Press.

Hawley, Willis D. (1981), 'Increasing the Effectiveness of School Desegregation: Lessons from Research'. In Adam Yarmolinsky et al., eds, *Race and Schooling in the City*, 145-62.

Hayles, Robert and Ronald W. Perry (1981), 'Racial Equality in the American Naval Justice System: An Analysis of Incarceration Differentials'. *Ethnic and Racial Studies*, 4,1: 44-55.

Heath, Anthony (1981), *Social Mobility*. London: Fontana.

Hechter, Michael (1975), *Internal Colonialism: The Celtic Fringe in British National Development, 1536-1966*. London: Routledge and Kegan Paul.

Hechter, Michael and Margaret Levi (1979), 'The Comparative Analysis of Ethnoregional Movements'. *Ethnic and Racial Studies*, 2,3: 260-74.

Heer, David (1980), 'Intermarriage'. In Stephan Thernstrom, ed. *Harvard Encyclopedia of American Ethnic Groups*, 513-21.

Heiberg, Marianne (1975), 'Insiders/Outsiders: Basque Nationalism'. *European Journal of Sociology*, 16: 169-93.

Hepple, Alexander (1967), *Verwoerd*. Harmondsworth: Penguin Books.

Hoetink, Hermannus (1967), *The Two Variants in Caribbean Race Relations*. London: Oxford University Press.

Homans, George (1964), 'Bringing Men Back In'. *American Sociological Review*, 29,6: 809-18.

Hope, Kempe R. and Maurice St Pierre (1983), 'Ethnic Political Participation and Cooperative Socialism in Guyana: A Critical Assessment'. *Ethnic and Racial Studies*, 6,4: 505-16.

Horowitz, Donald (1971), 'Three Dimensions of Ethnic Politics'. *World Politics*, 23: 232-44.

Horowitz, Donald (1985), 'Conflict and Conflict Management in a Multi-ethnic Society: Mexican-Americans in the Metropolis'. In Walker Connor, ed., *Mexican-Americans in Comparative Perspective*.

Horowitz, Irving L. (1980), *Taking Lives: Genocide and State Power*. New Brunswick, New Jersey: Transaction Books.

Hostetler, John A. (1980), *Amish Society*. (third edition) Ithaca: Cornell University Press.

Huber, Bettina (1981), 'Gutting Affirmative Action: New Policy in Action'. ASA *Footnotes* (December): 2-3.

Husbands, Christopher T. (1979), 'The "Threat" Hypothesis and Racist Voting in England and the United States'. In Robert Miles and Annie Phizacklea, eds, *Racism and Political Action in Britain*, 147-83.

Husbands, Christopher T. (1983), *Racial Exclusionism and the City: The Urban Support for the National Front*. London: Allen and Unwin.

Jay, Martin (1984), *Adorno*. London: Fontana.

Jensen, Arthur (1969), 'How Much Can We Boost IQ and Scholastic Achievement?'. *Harvard Educational Review*, 39: 1-123.

Jensen, Arthur (1980), *Bias in Mental Testing*. London: Methuen.

Kamin, Leon J. (1977), *The Science and Politics of IQ*. Harmondsworth: Penguin Books.

Karlovic, N.L. (1982), 'Internal Colonialism in a Marxist Society'. *Ethnic and Racial Studies*, 5,3: 276-99.

Karnig, Albert K. and Susan Welch (1980), *Black Representation and Urban Policy*. Chicago: University of Chicago Press.

Kawharu, I. Hugh (1977), *Maori Land Tenure: Studies in a Changing Institution*. Oxford: Clarendon Press.

Kennedy, Ruby J. (1944), 'Single or Triple Melting Pot? Intermarriage in New Haven, 1870-1940'. *American Journal of Sociology*, 49: 331-9.

Kennedy, Ruby J. (1952), 'Single or Triple Melting Pot? Intermarriage in New Haven, 1870-1950'. *American Journal of Sociology*, 58: 56-9.

Kerner, Otto (1968), *Report of the National Advisory Commission on Civil Disorders*. New York: Bantam.

Kerr, Clark (1984), *The Future of Industrial Societies: Convergence or Continuing Diversity?*. Cambridge, Mass: Harvard University Press.

Kerr, Clark, John T. Dunlop, Frederick H. Harbison and Charles A. Myers (1960), *Industrialism and Industrial Man*. London: Heinemann.

Killian, Lewis (1983), 'How Much Can Be Expected of Multicultural Education?'. *New Community*, 10,3: 421-3.

Kirk-Greene, Anthony H.M. (1980), '"Damnosa hereditas": Ethnic Ranking and the Martial Races Imperative in Africa'. *Ethnic and Racial Studies*, 3,4: 393-414.

Kirkwood, Kenneth (1965), *Britain and Africa*. London: Chatto and Windus.

Kirkwood, Kenneth (1983), 'The Dominant Minority'. *Journal of Biosocial Science*, 8: 129-53.

Kirp, David (1979), *Doing Good by Doing Little: Race and Schooling in Britain*. Berkeley: University of California Press.

Kofman, Eleonore (1982), 'Differential Modernization, Social Conflicts and Ethnoregionalism in Corsica'. *Ethnic and Racial Studies*, 5,3: 300-12.

Kolakowski, Leszek (1978), *Main Currents of Marxism: Its Rise, Growth, and Dissolution*. (three volumes) London: Oxford University Press.

Kowalewski, David (1981), 'National Rights Protests in the Brezhnev Era'. *Ethnic and Racial Studies*, 4,2: 175-87.

Kuhn, Thomas S. (1962), *The Structure of Scientific Revolutions*. Chicago: University of Chicago Press.

Kuper, Hilda (1969), 'Strangers in Plural Societies: Asians in South Africa and Uganda'. In Leo Kuper and M.G. Smith, eds, *Pluralism in Africa*, 247-82.

Kuper, Leo (1971a), 'Theories of Revolution and Race Relations'. *Comparative Studies in Society and History*, 13: 87-107. (Also reprinted in John Stone, ed. (1977), *Race, Ethnicity and Social Change*, 178-96.)

Kuper, Leo (1971b), 'Political Change in Plural Societies: Problems in Racial Pluralism'. *International Social Science Journal*, 23,4: 594-607.

Kuper, Leo (1981), *Genocide*. Harmondsworth: Penguin Books.

Kuper, Leo and M.G. Smith, eds (1969), *Pluralism in Africa*. Berkeley: University of California Press.

Lal, Barbara (1983), 'Perspectives on Ethnicity: Old Wine in New Bottles'. *Ethnic and Racial Studies*, 6,1: 154-73.

Lamar, Howard and Leonard Thompson, eds (1981), *The Frontier in History: North America and South Africa Compared*. New Haven: Yale University Press.

Layton-Henry, Zig (1984), *The Politics of Race in Britain*. London: George Allen and Unwin.

Lee, Changsoo and George de Vos (1982), *Koreans in Japan: Ethnic Conflict and Accommodation*. Berkeley and Los Angeles: University of California Press.

Lee, Yong L. (1983), 'Ethnic Differences and the State-Minority Relationship in Southeast Asia'. *Ethnic and Racial Studies*, 6,2: 213-20.

Lenin, Vladimir I. (1942), 'Imperialism and the Split in the Socialist Movement'. In *Collected Works*, volume 19 (1916-17), 337-51. Moscow: Foreign Publishing House.

Lever, Henry (1978), *South African Society*. Johannesburg: Jonathan Ball.

Lieberson, Stanley (1961), 'A Societal Theory of Race and Ethnic Relations'. *American Sociological Review*, 26,6: 902-10.

Lieberson, Stanley (1980), *A Piece of the Pie: Blacks and White Immigrants Since 1880*. Berkeley and Los Angeles: University of California Press.

Lijphart, Arend (1968), *The Politics of Accommodation: Pluralism and Democracy in the Netherlands*. Berkeley: University of California Press.

Lijphart, Arend (1977), *Democracy in Plural Societies: A Comparative Exploration*. New Haven: Yale University Press.

Lim, Mah H. (1985), 'Affirmative Action, Ethnicity and Integration: The Case of Malaysia'. *Ethnic and Racial Studies*, 8,2: 250-76.

Lind, Andrew W. (1969), *Hawaii: The Last of the Magic Isles*. London: Oxford University Press.

Little, Alan and Diana Robbins (1982), *'Loading the Law': A Study of Transmitted Deprivation, Ethnic Minorities and Affirmative Action*. London: Commission for Racial Equality.

Little, Alan and Richard Willey (1981), *Multi-ethnic Education: The Way Forward*. Schools Council Report No. 18.

Llobera, Josep R. (1983), 'The Idea of *Volksgeist* in the Formation of Catalan Nationalist Ideology'. *Ethnic and Racial Studies*, 6,3: 332-50.

Lockwood, David (1970), 'Race, Conflict and Plural Society'. In Sami Zubaida, ed., *Race and Racialism*, 57-72. London: Tavistock.

Louden, Delroy (1981), 'A Comparative Study of Self-Concepts Among Minority and Majority Group Adolescents in English Multi-Racial Schools'. *Ethnic and Racial Studies*, 4,2: 153-74.

Low-Hang, Kathleen (1984), 'Colour and Class Inequality in Seychelles'. Unpublished Ph.D: University of Bristol.

Lustgarten, Lawrence (1980), *Legal Control of Racial Discrimination*. London: Macmillan.

Lyon, Judson (1980), 'Marxism and Ethno-nationalism in Guinea-Bissau, 1956-76'. *Ethnic and Racial Studies*, 3,2: 156-68.

Marcuse, Herbert (1964), *One Dimensional Man*. Boston: Beacon.

Marcuse, Herbert (1969), *An Essay on Liberation*. Boston: Beacon.

Marcuse, Herbert (1972), *Counterrevolution and Revolt*. Boston: Beacon.

Mason, David (1982), 'Race Relations, Group Formation and Power: A Framework for Analysis'. *Ethnic and Racial Studies*, 5,4: 421-39.

Mason, Philip (1970), *Patterns of Dominance*. London: Oxford University Press.

Mazrui, Ali (1978), 'Negritude, the Talmudic Tradition and Intellectual Performance of Blacks and Jews'. *Ethnic and Racial Studies*, 1,1: 19-36.

McAllister, Ian and Anthony Mughan (1984), 'The Fate of the Language: Determinants of Bilingualism in Wales'. *Ethnic and Racial Studies*, 7,3: 321-41.

McCrudden, Christopher (1983), 'Anti-discrimination Goals and the Legal Process'. In Nathan Glazer and Ken Young, eds, *Ethnic Pluralism and Public Policy*, 55-74.

McKay, David H. (1977), *Housing and Race in Industrial Society: Civil Rights and Urban Policy in Britain and the United States*. London: Croom Helm.

McKay, James and Frank Lewins (1978), 'Ethnicity and the Ethnic Group: A Conceptual Analysis and Reformulation'. *Ethnic and Racial Studies*, 1,4: 412-27.

McLellan, David (1975), *Marx*. London: Fontana.

McRoberts, Kenneth (1979), 'Internal Colonialism: The Case of Quebec'. *Ethnic and Racial Studies*, 2,3: 293-318.

Mennell, Stephen (1980), *Sociological Theory: Uses and Unities*. (second edition) London: Nelson.

Merton, Robert K. (1941), 'Intermarriage and the Social Structure: Fact and Theory'. *Psychiatry*, 4: 361-74.

Merton, Robert K. (1949), 'Discrimination and the American Creed'. In R.M. MacIver, ed., *Discrimination and National Welfare*. New York: Harper and Row.

Miles, Robert (1980), 'Class, Race and Ethnicity: A Critique of Cox's Theory'. *Ethnic and Racial Studies*, 3,2: 169-87.

Miles, Robert (1984). 'Marxism versus the Sociology of Race Relations'. *Ethnic and Racial Studies*, 7,2: 217-37.

Miles, Robert and Annie Phizacklea (1979), *Racism and Political Action in Britain*. London: Routledge and Kegan Paul.

Moodie, Dunbar T. (1975), *The Rise of Afrikanerdom*. Berkeley: University of California Press.

Moodley, Kogila (1983), 'Canadian Multi-culturalism as Ideology'. *Ethnic and Racial Studies*, 6,3: 320-31.

Morin, Françoise (1982), *Indianité Ethnocide Indigenisme en Amérique Latine*. Paris: Editions du CNRS.

Moskos, Charles C. (1980), 'Who Remembers the Armenians?'. *Contemporary Sociology*, 9,4: 493-5.

Mughan, Anthony (1979), 'Modernization and Regional Relative Deprivation: Towards a Theory of Ethnic Conflict'. In L.J. Sharpe, ed., *Decentralist Trends in Western Democracies*. London: Sage.

Mughan, Anthony and Ian McAllister (1981), 'The Mobilization of the Ethnic Vote: A Thesis with some Scottish and Welsh Evidence'. *Ethnic and Racial Studies*, 4,2: 189-204.

Myrdal, Gunnar (1944), *An American Dilemma: The Negro Problem and Modern Democracy*. New York: Harper and Row.

Nicholls, David (1981), '"No Hawkers and Pedlars": Levantines in the Caribbean'. *Ethnic and Racial Studies*, 4,4: 415-31.

Noel, Donald L. (1968), 'A Theory of the Origin of Ethnic Stratification'. *Social Problems*, 16,2: 157-72.

Norton, Robert (1977), *Race and Politics in Fiji*. St Lucia: University of Queensland Press.

Novak, Michael (1971), *The Rise of the Unmeltable Ethnics*. New York: Macmillan.

Okamura, Jonathan Y. (1981), 'Situational Ethnicity'. *Ethnic and Racial Studies*, 4,4: 452-65.

Olzak, Susan (1982), 'Ethnic Mobilization in Quebec'. *Ethnic and Racial Studies*, 5,3: 253-75.

Orfield, Gary (1978), *Must We Bus?: Segregated Schools and National Policy*. Washington DC: Brookings Institution.

Orfield, Gary (1981), 'Why it Worked in Dixie: Southern School Desegregation and its Implications for the North'. In Adam Yarmolinsky et al., eds, *Race and Schooling in the City*, 24-44.

Painter, Nell I. (1979), *The Narrative of Hosea Hudson: His Life as a Negro Communist in the South*. Cambridge, Mass: Harvard University Press.

Pareto, Vilfredo (1902), *Les Systèmes Socialistes*. In S.E. Finer, ed. (1966), *Vilfredo Pareto: Sociological Writings*, 123-42.

Pareto, Vilfredo (1916), *Trattato di Sociologia Generale*. In S.E.Finer, ed. (1966), *Vilfredo Pareto: Sociological Writings*, 167-250.

Park, Robert E. and Ernest W. Burgess (1921), *Introduction to the Science of Sociology*. Chicago: Chicago University Press.

Parkin, Frank (1979), *Marxism and Class Theory: A Bourgeois Critique*. London: Tavistock.

Parsons, Talcott (1966), *Societies: Evolutionary and Comparative Perspectives.* Englewood Cliffs, NJ: Prentice-Hall.

Patterson, Orlando (1977), *Ethnic Chauvinism: The Reactionary Impulse.* New York: Stein and Day.

Patterson, Orlando (1984), *Slavery and Social Death: A Comparative Study.* Cambridge, Mass: Harvard University Press.

Peach, Ceri (1980), 'Which Triple Melting Pot?'. *Ethnic and Racial Studies,* 3,1: 1-16.

Peel, John D.Y. (1969), 'Spencer and the Neo-Evolutionists'. *Sociology,* 3,2: 173-91.

Pereira, Cecil, Bert N. Adams and Mike Bristow (1978), 'Canadian Beliefs and Policy Regarding the Admission of Ugandan Asians to Canada'. *Ethnic and Racial Studies,* 1,3: 352-64.

Peres, Yochanan and Ruth Schrift (1978), 'Intermarriage and Interethnic Relations: A Comparative Study'. *Ethnic and Racial Studies,* 1,4: 428-51.

Pettigrew, Thomas F. (1971), *Racially Separate or Together?.* New York: McGraw-Hill. (Also reprinted in John Stone, ed. (1977), *Race, Ethnicity and Social Change,* 375-99.)

Pettigrew, Thomas F. (1981), 'The Case for Metropolitan Approaches to Public School Desegregation'. In Adam Yarmolinsky et al., eds, *Race and Schooling in the City,* 163-81.

Pettigrew, Thomas F. and R. Green (1976), 'School Desegregation in Large Cities: A Critique of the Coleman "White Flight" Thesis'. *Harvard Educational Review,* 46: 225-33.

Phizacklea, Annie and Robert Miles (1980), *Labour and Racism.* London: Routledge and Kegan Paul.

Pinkney, Alphonso (1984), *The Myth of Black Progress.* Cambridge: Cambridge University Press.

Pipes, Richard (1975), 'Reflections on the Nationality Problems in the Soviet Union'. In Nathan Glazer and Daniel P. Moynihan, eds, *Ethnicity: Theory and Experience,* 453-65.

Pitt-Rivers, Julian (1973), 'Race in Latin America: The Concept of "Raza"'. *European Journal of Sociology,* 14: 12-31.

Poulantzas, N. (1975), *Classes in Contemporary Capitalism.* London: New Left Books.

Pye, Lucian W. (1975), 'China: Ethnic Minorities and National Security'. In Nathan Glazer and Daniel P. Moynihan, eds, *Ethnicity: Theory and Experience,* 489-512.

Rabushka, Alvin and Kenneth A. Shepsle (1972), *Politics in Plural Societies: A Theory of Democratic Instability.* Columbus, Ohio: Merrill.

Ray, John J. (1981), 'Explaining Australian Attitudes Towards Aborigines'. *Ethnic and Racial Studies*, 4,3: 348-52.

Ray, John J. and Adrian Furnham (1984), 'Authoritarianism, Conservatism and Racism'. *Ethnic and Racial Studies*, 7,3: 406-12.

Reed, John S. (1980), 'Sociology and Regional Studies in the United States'. *Ethnic and Racial Studies*, 3,1: 40-51.

Reed, John S. (1982), *One South: An Ethnic Approach to Regional Culture*. Baton Rouge: Louisiana State University Press.

Reid, John (1982), 'Black America in the 1980s'. In *Daily Telegraph*, 30 December.

Rex, John (1970), *Race Relations in Sociological Theory*. London: Weidenfeld and Nicolson.

Rex, John (1979), 'Review of Harrison M. Wright's *The Burden of the Present*'. *Ethnic and Racial Studies*, 2,2: 246-7.

Rex, John (1981), 'A Working Paradigm for Race Relations Research'. *Ethnic and Racial Studies*, 4,1: 1-25.

Rex, John and Robert Moore (1967), *Race, Community and Conflict: A Study of Sparkbrook*. London: Oxford University Press.

Rex, John and Sally Tomlinson (1979), *Colonial Immigrants in a British City: A Class Analysis*. London: Routledge and Kegan Paul.

Reynolds, Henry (1982), *The Other Side of the Frontier: Aboriginal Resistance to the European Invasion of Australia*. Harmondsworth: Penguin Books.

Reynolds, Vernon (1980), 'Sociobiology and the Idea of Primordial Discrimination'. *Ethnic and Racial Studies*, 3,3: 303-15.

Richmond, Anthony H., ed. (1984), 'After the Referenda: The Future of Ethnic Nationalism in Britain and Canada'. *Ethnic and Racial Studies*, 7,1: 1-193.

Rist, Ray C. (1979), 'Guestworkers in Germany: Public Policies as the Legitimation of Marginality'. *Ethnic and Racial Studies*, 2,4: 401-15.

Roof, Wade C. (1978), '"The Negro as an Immigrant Group": A Research Note on Chicago's Racial Trends'. *Ethnic and Racial Studies*, 1,4: 452-64.

Rose, E.J.B. et al. (1969), *Colour and Citizenship: A Report on British Race Relations*. London: Oxford University Press.

Rose, Steven, Leon J. Kamin and R.C. Lewontin (1984), *Not in our Genes: Biology, Ideology and Human Nature*. Harmondsworth: Penguin Books.

Ross, Robert (1983), *Cape of Torments: Slavery and Resistance in South Africa*. London: Routledge and Kegan Paul.

Rothchild, Donald and Victor A. Olorunsola, eds (1982), *State Versus Ethnic Claims: African Policy Dilemmas*. Boulder, Colorado: Westview Press.

Sahlins, Marshall (1976), *The Uses and Abuses of Biology*. Ann Arbor: University of Michigan Press.

Scarman, Lord (1981), *The Brixton Disorders, 10-12 April 1981*. Cmnd. 8427, London: Her Majesty's Stationery Office.

Schermerhorn, Richard A. (1970), *Comparative Ethnic Relations*. New York: Random House.

Schmitter, Barbara E. (1983), 'Immigrant Minorities in West Germany: Some Theoretical Concerns'. *Ethnic and Racial Studies*, 6,3: 308-19.

Segal, Ronald (1966), *The Race War*. London: Jonathan Cape.

Seton-Watson, Hugh (1982), 'The History of Nations'. *The Times Higher Education Supplement*, 27 August: 12-13.

Shils, Edward (1957), 'Primordial, Personal, Sacred and Civil Ties'. *British Journal of Sociology*, 8: 130-45.

Simmel, Georg (1977), 'The Stranger'. In John Stone, ed., *Race, Ethnicity and Social Change*, 13-17.

Simons, H.J. and R.E. Simons (1969), *Class and Colour in South Africa, 1850-1950*. Harmondsworth: Penguin Books.

Sithole, Masipula (1980), 'Ethnicity and Factionalism in Zimbabwe Nationalist Politics, 1957-79'. *Ethnic and Racial Studies*, 3,1: 17-39.

Smelser, Neil (1963), *Theory of Collective Behavior*. New York: Free Press.

Smith, Anthony D. (1981a), 'War and Ethnicity: The Role of Warfare in the Formation, Self-images and Cohesion of Ethnic Communities'. *Ethnic and Racial Studies*, 4,4: 375-97.

Smith, Anthony D. (1981b), *The Ethnic Revival in the Modern World*. Cambridge: Cambridge University Press.

Smith, Anthony D. (1983), *State and Nation in the Third World*. Brighton: Wheatsheaf Books.

Smith, David J. (1977), *Racial Disadvantage in Britain: The PEP Report*. Harmondsworth: Penguin Books.

Smith, Michael G. (1965), *The Plural Society in the British West Indies*. Berkeley: University of California Press.

Smith, Michael G. (1982), 'Ethnicity and Ethnic Groups in America: The View from Harvard'. *Ethnic and Racial Studies*, 5,1: 1-22.

Srinivas, M.N. (1969), 'The Caste System in India'. In André Béteille, ed., *Social Inequality*, 265-72. Harmondsworth: Penguin Books.

Steinberg, Stephen (1981), *The Ethnic Myth: Race, Ethnicity, and Class in America*. New York: Atheneum.

Steiner, Jurg and Jeffrey Obler (1977), 'Does the Consociational Theory Really Hold for Switzerland?'. In Milton Esman, ed., *Ethnic Conflict in the Western World*, 324-42.

Stone, John (1973), *Colonist or Uitlander?: A Study of the British Immigrant in South Africa*. Oxford: Clarendon Press.

Stone, John (1975), 'The Migrant Factor in a Plural Society'. *International Migration Review*, 9,1: 15-29.

Stone, John (1976), 'Black Nationalism and Apartheid: Two Variations on a Separatist Theme'. *Social Dynamics*, 2,1: 19-31.

Stone, John, ed. (1977), *Race, Ethnicity and Social Change*. California: Wadsworth.

Stone, John (1978), 'Review of Oliver C. Cox's *Race Relations*'. *Ethnic and Racial Studies*, 1,1: 129-30.

Stone, John (1979), 'Internal Colonialism in Comparative Perspective'. *Ethnic and Racial Studies*, 2,3: 255-9.

Stone, John (1982), 'Ethnicity versus the State: The Dual Claims of State Coherence and Ethnic Self-Determination'. In Donald Rothchild and Victor Olorunsola, eds, *State Versus Ethnic Claims: African Policy Dilemmas*, 85-99.

Stone, John (1985), 'Ethnicity and Stratification: Mexican-Americans and European *Gastarbeiter* in Comparative Perspective'. In Walker Connor, ed., *Mexican-Americans in Comparative Perspective*.

Stone, John and Stephen Mennell (1980), *Alexis de Tocqueville on Democracy, Revolution and Society*. Chicago: Chicago University Press.

Stone, Maureen (1981), *The Education of the Black Child in Britain: The Myth of Multicultural Education*. London: Fontana.

Stryker, Sheldon (1974), '"A Theory of Middleman Minorities" – A Comment'. *American Sociological Review*, 39,2: 281-2.

Svensson, Frances (1978), 'The Final Crisis of Tribalism: Comparative Ethnic Policy on American and Russian Frontiers'. *Ethnic and Racial Studies*, 1,1: 100-23.

Taeuber, Karl E. and Alma F. Taeuber (1965), *Negroes in Cities*. Chicago: Aldine.

Taeuber, Karl E. and Franklin D. Wilson (1979), 'Report on the impact of the type and character of desegregation programs on school desegregation'. Madison: Institute for Research on Poverty, University of Wisconsin.

Tatz, Colin (1980), 'Aborigines, Law and Race Relations'. *Ethnic and Racial Studies*, 3,3: 281-302.

Tatz, Colin (1983), *Aborigines and Uranium and Other Essays*. Australia: Heinemann Educational.

Taylor, Howard F. (1981), *The IQ Game: A Methodological Inquiry into the Heredity-Environment Controversy*. Brighton: Harvester Press.

Taylor, Stan (1979), 'The National Front: Anatomy of a Political Movement'. In Robert Miles and Annie Phizacklea, eds, *Racism and Political Action in Britain*, 124-46.

Thernstrom, Stephan, ed. (1980), *The Harvard Encyclopedia of American Ethnic Groups*. Cambridge, Mass: Harvard University Press.

Thomas, Colin J. and Colin H. Williams (1978), 'Language and Nationalism in Wales'. *Ethnic and Racial Studies*, 1,2: 235-58.

Thomas, W.I. and Florian Znaniecki (1918-20), *The Polish Peasant in Europe and America*. Chicago and Boston: Richard G. Badger.

Thompson, John L.P. (1983), 'The Plural Society Approach to Class and Ethnic Political Mobilization'. *Ethnic and Racial Studies*, 6,2: 127-53.

Thornberry, Patrick (1980), 'Minority Rights, Human Rights and International Law'. *Ethnic and Racial Studies*, 3,3: 249-63.

Tingsten, Herbert (1979), 'National Self-Examination' (trans. Michael Banton). *Ethnic and Racial Studies*, 2,1: 38-54.

Tinker, Hugh (1977), *Race, Conflict and the International Order: From Empire to United Nations*. London: Macmillan.

Tocqueville, Alexis de (1966), *The Ancien Régime and the French Revolution* (trans. Stuart Gilbert). London: Collins.

Tomlinson, Sally (1981), *Educational Subnormality: A Study in Decision-Making*. London: Routledge and Kegan Paul.

Turner, Jonathan and Edna Bonacich (1980), 'Toward a Composite Theory of Middleman Minorities'. *Ethnicity*, 7: 144-58.

Udalagama, D.B. (1982), 'Sri Lanka to Operate Ethnic Quota System'. *The Times Higher Education Supplement*, 6 August 1982.

van Amersfoort, J.M.M. (1978), 'Minority as a Sociological Concept'. *Ethnic and Racial Studies*, 1,2: 218-34.

van Amersfoort, J.M.M. (1982), *Immigration and Minority Group Formation: The Dutch Experience, 1945-75*. Cambridge: Cambridge University Press.

van Amersfoort, J.M.M., Philip Muus and Rinus Penninx (1984), 'International Migration, the Economic Crisis and the State: An Analysis of Mediterranean Migration to Western Europe'. *Ethnic and Racial Studies*, 7,2: 238-68.

van Amersfoort, J.M.M. and Herman van der Wusten (1981), 'Democratic Stability and Ethnic Parties'. *Ethnic and Racial Studies*, 4,4: 476-85.

van den Berghe, Pierre L. (1965), *South Africa: A Study in Conflict*. Middletown, Connecticut: Wesleyan University Press.

van den Berghe, Pierre L. (1974), 'Bringing Beasts Back In: Toward a Biosocial Theory of Aggression'. *American Sociological Review*, 39,6: 777-88.

van den Berghe, Pierre L. (1978a), *Race and Racism: A Comparative Perspective*. (second edition) New York: John Wiley.

van den Berghe, Pierre L. (1978b), 'Race and Ethnicity: A Sociobiological Perspective'. *Ethnic and Racial Studies*, 1,4: 401-11.

van den Berghe, Pierre L. (1981), *The Ethnic Phenomenon*. New York: Elsevier.

van Valey, Thomas L., Wade C. Roof and Jerome E. Wilcox (1977), 'Trends in Residential Segregation, 1960-70'. *American Journal of Sociology*, 82: 826-44.

Wai, Dunstan (1978), 'Sources of Communal Conflicts and Secessionist Politics in Africa'. *Ethnic and Racial Studies*, 1,3: 286-305.

Wallerstein, Immanuel (1974), *The Modern World System*. New York: Academic Press.

Ward, Robin (1979), 'Where Race Didn't Divide: Some Reflections on Slum Clearance in Manchester'. In Robert Miles and Annie Phizacklea, eds, *Racism and Political Action in Britain*, 204-22.

Weber, Max (1930), *The Protestant Ethic and the Spirit of Capitalism* (trans. Talcott Parsons). London: George Allen and Unwin.

Wilson, Edward O. (1975), *Sociobiology: The New Synthesis*. Cambridge, Mass: Harvard University Press.

Wilson, William J. (1978), *The Declining Significance of Race: Blacks and Changing American Institutions*. Chicago: Chicago University Press.

Wirsing, Robert G., ed. (1981), *Protection of Ethnic Minorities: Comparative Perspectives*. New York and Oxford: Pergamon Press.

Wirth, Louis (1945), 'The Problem of Minority Groups'. In Ralph Linton, ed., *The Science of Man in the World Crisis*, 347-72. New York: Columbia University Press.

Woods, Robert (1979), 'Ethnic Segregation in Birmingham in the 1960s and 1970s'. *Ethnic and Racial Studies*, 2,3: 455-76.

Wright, Harrison M. (1977), *The Burden of the Present: Liberal-Radical Controversy over Southern African History*. Cape Town: David Philip.

Yarmolinsky, Adam, Lance Liebman and Corinne S. Schelling, eds (1981), *Race and Schooling in the City*. Cambridge, Mass: Harvard University Press.

Young, Crawford (1976), *The Politics of Cultural Pluralism*. Madison: University of Wisconsin Press.

Young, Crawford (1982), 'Comparative Claims to Political Sovereignty: Biafra, Katanga, Eritrea'. In Donald Rothchild and Victor Olorunsola, eds, *State Versus Ethnic Claims: African Policy Dilemmas*, 199-232.

Zenner, Walter P. (1982), 'Arabic-speaking Immigrants in North America as Middleman Minorities'. *Ethnic and Racial Studies*, 5,4: 457-77.

Index

Aborigines, Australian 13, 16, 53,
  143-4
Adam, H. 68
Adorno, T. 28-30
affirmative action programmes 10, 16,
  101, 147-52
Affirmative Discrimination 148-51
Allotment Act of 1887 143
*American Dilemma, An: the Negro
  Problem and Modern Democracy* 27
Amersfoort, J.M.M. van 19, 44-7
Anglo-conformity 138-9
apartheid 9-10, 15-16, 43, 135, 141
  and group identification 36-7, 39
  Marxist analysis of 65-9
Australia and Aborigines 13, 16, 53,
  143-4
Authoritarian Personality, The 28-9
Avineri, S. 63

Banton, M. 60
Berghe, P. v.d. 31-2, 49-52, 160
Beyond the Melting Pot 150
bilingualism and education 117-18,
  122-5
biological theories of race 17-18, 20,
  62, 157
  kin selection 31-3
Black Muslims 10, 139
black studies programmes 123, 125
Blalock, H.M. 47-8
Blauner, R. 64-5
Blumer, H. 66, 84-7
Bogardus social distance test 110-11
Bonacich, E. 67-8, 96-8
Brown v. (US) Board of Education 10,
  118, 132
Bulmer, M. 26
Burman, S. 132-3

Burt, Sir C. 31
busing *see* school busing

Cabral, A. 79-81
Canada and Quebec nationalism 13,
  89, 101
Carey, A.T. 127
Caste and Class in a Southern Town 26
Caste, Class and Race 29-30, 71
Castles, S. and Kosack, G. 69
centralization, state and
  ethno-nationalism 105-6, 109
Chicago School (of Sociology) 18, 24-6,
  48-9, 128-9
China and ethnic minorities 12, 77-8
Chinese as middlemen 95, 98, 100
Civil Rights Act 131
Civil Rights movement 10
class-based theories and race
  relations 30, 57-60, 62-73, 81, 84
Classes in Contemporary Capitalism 70
Cohen, G. 125
colonial(ism) 9-10
  conquest and race relations 52-5, 58
  and genocide 155-6
  and plural societies 91-6
  policies in Africa 12-13, 80, 100
  and social structure 57-9
Colonial Policy and Practice 92
colour tax 127
Commission for Racial Equality 130-1
Communist parties and black
  workers 65-6, 71-2
competitive models of ethnic
  mobilization 107-9
Connor, W. 84, 87-91
consociation 93, 145-7
convergence theory 84
Cooley, C. 24

Cox, O.C.   29-30, 71
cultural imperialism   90

Declining Significance of Race, The   16
Democracy in America   22
democracy, consociational   145-7
democracy and pluralism   144-7
desegregation   118-21
Deutsch, K.   87-8
differential incorporation   93
discrimination *see* apartheid, ethnicity,
    minorities, race, working-class
    racism
discrimination, positive   16, 42, 55,
    147-52
Dollard, J.   26
Dreyer, J.   78
Du Bois, W.E.B.   25
Duncan, O.   130-1
Durkheim, E.   19-20, 23
Dworkin, R.   151

economic factors
    and intermarriage   114-15
    and race relations   14-15, 61, 72,
        106-7, 130-3, 137
    overemphasis on   61, 79, 81-2, 89,
        103, 157
education for barbarism   117
education and race relations   117-26
élites and subordinated masses   44, 58,
    94-7
embourgeoisement theory   84
employment and race relations   130-2
Encausse, H.C. d'   64
Engels, F.   64
*Essay on the Inequality of the Human
    Races*   21-2
ethnic(ity)
    barriers and industrialization   84,
        107-8
    consciousness   43, 69, 87-8
    and marriage   113-16
    and war   152-4
    definitions of 19
    groups
        in plural societies   93-4
        and racial groups   34-6
        and social change   87-91

identity and state loyalty   90-1
    of last resort   11
    middlemen   95-100
    nationalism   73-81, 87, 89, 104-9
    revivals   11, 15, 16, 90, 100-9
    studies programmes   123-5
    symbolic   102-3
    white ethnics   10, 100-3, 149
    see also minorities; race
Eysenck, H.   17

family and race relations   110-17
Fanon, F.   54, 63
'figment of pigment'   34
'final solution'   36
Fitzhugh, G.   24
Frankfurt School   63
Frazier, E.F.   24
Furnivall, J.S.   91-3, 95

Gans, H.   40-1, 102-3
Galton, F.   23, 24
Gastarbeiter   11
genetic determinism   17-18, 24, 30-1
genocide   46, 53-4, 152, 154-7
Genovese, E.   72-3
Glazer, N. and Moynihan, D.P.   101-2,
    148-51
Gobineau, A. de   21-4, 31
Goldhagen, E.   74
Great Depression   71
Greeley, A.   15
Guinea-Bissau and ethnic
    minorities   79-81

Harris, M.   72
Hechter, M.   107
Heer, D.   114
heterogeneous societies   92-3
homogeneous societies   87-92
'honorary Aryans'   36-7
'honorary whites'   36
Horowitz, D.   34
Horowitz, I.   154-5
housing and race relations   126-30
Hughes, H.   24
hypergamy/hypogamy   116

immigrants

in Europe 11-12, 52, 59, 69-70
to US 52, 138
and US blacks 39-42, 59, 150
Immigrant Workers and Class Structure in Western Europe 69
Indian caste system and marriage 111-12
Indians as middlemen 96, 98, 100
indigenous populations
  and introduced ethnic groups 54-5
  sociological 53
  subordination of 52-6, 65-8, 73-81
institutional discrimination 28-9, 38, 103, 147-8
'intelligence' tests 17-18, 21, 30-1
intermarriage *see* marriage
internal colonialism 72, 79, 107, 140
Introduction to the Science of Sociology 25
IQ controversies 17-18, 21, 30-1
Ireland, Northern, as plural society 94

Japan and Burakumin 13, 36
Jensen, A. 17
Jews
  and black quotas (US) 41-2
  genocide of 14, 154
  identification of 36
  as middlemen 96, 98, 100
  as oppressed minority 51-2, 73-4
job reservation 67, 86
Johnson, C.S. 26

Karlovic, N.L. 79
Kennedy, R. 113
kin selection 31-3
Kuhn, T. 31
Kuper, L. 155

Labour and Racism 70
labour market, split 66-8, 115
Lau v. Nichols 124
Lenin 64, 74, 75
Lieberson, S. 49, 52-7
Lijphart, A. 145-6
Lyon, J. 80

majority attitudes and minorities 44-7, 137

Marcuse, H. 63, 72
marriage
  and group boundaries 110-13
  interethnic 113-16
  interracial 112-14
Marx, K. 62, 136
  and capitalism 43, 60, 63-4, 74
  and minorities 20, 75
Marxism
  analysis of apartheid 65-9
  and minority groups in socialist states 73-82
  'open' and 'vulgar' 64, 73, 81
  perspectives on race relations 62-5, 71-3
  and working-class racialism 69-73
Mazrui, A. 41
'melting pot' theory 10-11, 138-9
Merton, R.K. 29
middlemen 13, 58, 95-100, 156
migrant
  domination/subordination 53-6
  workers in Europe 11, 52, 69-70
  and see immigrants
minorities 10-12
  concentrated and dispersed 45-7, 117-22, 129
  definition of 42-3
  and education 117-26
  and employment 130-2
  goals 44-5
  and housing 126-30
  identification of 35-7
  middlemen 13, 58, 95-100, 156
  and modernization 84-91
  and power 37-8, 42-5, 99-100, 134
  rights 44, 46, 137
  in socialist societies 12, 73-81
  tribal 141-4
  urban 126-32, 148-51
miscegenation, social results of 112-13
mobility and status 84-6
modernization theory of race relations 83-91, 107-9
Mughan, A. 107-8
multicultural education 117-18, 123-5
Myrdal, G. 27, 29, 30

nationalism

definitions of   89-91
see also ethnicity
nation-building   84, 88-91
nation-states   11-12, 87-91
Negro in Chicago, The   26
New Zealand and ethnic minorities   13
Noel, D.   48

On the Jewish Question   74

Pareto, V.   27
Park, R.E. and Burgess, E.W.   24-5, 48, 52, 56
Parkin, F.   65
Parsons, T.   50
passing as white   112
paternalism and race relations   49-52
Patterson, O.   15
Peach, C.   113
Peres, Y. and Schrift, R.   114-16
Pettigrew, T.   119, 139-40
Phizacklea, A. and Miles, R.   70-1
physical mobility and racial order   86
Plekhanov   74
plural societies   44, 91-100, 135
   and democracy   144-7
   ethnic pluralism   138-9
   and genocide   156
   new pluralists   103
policy space   143
Polish Peasant in Europe and America   24-5
political power and race relations   132-4
Poulantzas, N.   70
positive discrimination   16, 42, 55, 147-52
power
   analysis of race relations   27-8
   balance
      and injustice   136, 144-7, 156
      and modernization   108-9
      and minority groups   37-8, 42-5, 157-8
   political   132-4
   and race relations   19, 37-8, 47-61, 81-2, 99-100, 134
   and resources   47-8, 117, 121, 128-9
primordial ties   14, 15, 32-3, 106
Pye, L.   77

quotas
   education and employment   41-2, 55, 126
   and racial justice   147-52, 157-8

Rabushka, A. and Shepsle, K.   145-6
race/racial
   barriers and industrialization   66-8, 84-7
   consciousness   43, 70
   definitions and social consequences   21-4, 31
   discrimination in
      education   118-26
      employment   126, 130-2
      housing   126-30
   division and war   152-4
   groups
      and ethnic groups   34-6
      and pluralism   91-4
   integration   118-21
   justice   43-4, 136-58
   middlemen   95-100
   theorizing   17-26, 31-3, 62, 157
race relations
   army and   134-5
   education and   117-26
   etiquette of   51
   family and   110-17
   ideologies of   137-44
   Marxist models   49-60
   modernization theory   83-91, 107-9
   police and   134-5
   political parties and (UK)   133-4
   rational choice theory   60
   see also economic factors; power
Race Relations Act   131, 151
Race Relations Board   122
Race War, The   153
racialism/racism
   communist   65-6, 71-2
   and fascism   27, 28, 133-4
   justifications for   60
   political parties and (UK)   133-4
   reverse   16, 148
   sociology and   17-26, 31-3
   in US   16, 71-3, 119, 134
   working-class   30, 69, 73, 101-2
   see also apartheid; race discrimination

Rex, J. 49, 57-60, 70
and Moore, R. 128-9
Reynolds, V. 33
Rules of Sociological Method 23
Russia *see* USSR
Russians, ethnic 12, 75-7, 135

Sahlins, M. 33
Schermerhorn, R. 44
school
busing 101, 117-22
curriculum 122-5
Segal, R. 153
separatism 10, 90, 139-44, 157
defensive 16
of middlemen minorities 97
nationalism and 104-9
see also apartheid
Seton-Watson, H. 82
Simmel, G. 96
Smith, A. 153
Smith, M.G. 92-3
social change and race relations 83-91,
107-9, 126
social mobility and status 84-6
social repute and group
identification 39
socialist societies and ethnic
minorities 12, 73-81
sociobiology 31-3
Sociobiology: the New Synthesis 31-2
sociology and race theories 16-26, 31-3
sojourning 96-100
South Africa
apartheid 9-10, 15-16, 43, 135, 141
group identification 36-7, 39
Marxist analysis of 65-9
Cape Coloureds 39, 58, 112
South/Central America
and class-based theories 81
Indians 14, 16, 136
Sri-Lanka and Tamils 151-2
Stalin, J. 12
and minorities 64, 74-6
state-building 87-91
stateless nations 109

Sternberg, S. 103
Stone, A.H. 25
'stranger' hypothesis 49
Stranger, The 96
stratification
ethnic/racial 26-7, 58, 89, 110-11
social 42, 57-9, 71
*Structure of Scientific Revolutions,
The* 31
Sumner, W.G. 24
Svensson, F. 16, 141-3

Tatz, C. 143-4
Thomas, W.I. 18
and Znaniecki, F. 24-5
Tocqueville, A. de 10, 22-4, 31, 43
Toënnies F. 50
Treatise on General Sociology, The 27
tribalism and separatism 141-4
tribal peoples and genocide 154-6

United Nations 9
universalism 16, 93
USSR
and ethnic minorities 12, 74-7, 141-3
Native Code of 1822 142

vertical mosaic 13
Voting Rights Act (US) 132

Wallerstein, I. 57
war and ethnic/racial divisions 14,
152-4
Ward, L. 24
WASP establishment (US) 138
Weber, M. 20-1, 50, 60
White Anglo-Saxon Protestants 138
White Australia policy 13
'white flight' 119, 126
Wilson, W.J. 16
Wirth, L. 42-4
working-class racism
in Europe 69-73
in South Africa 65-8
in US 71-3, 101-2
Wretched of the Earth, The 54